How to Select Stocks Using Technical Analysis

Martin J. Pring on Technical Analysis Series

Momentum Explained, volume I
Candlesticks Explained
Technician's Guide to Day and Swing Trading
Momentum Explained, volume II
Breaking the Black Box

How to Select Stocks Using Technical Analysis

Martin J. Pring

McGraw-Hill
New York   Chicago   San Francisco
Lisbon   London   Madrid   Mexico City   Milan
New Delhi   San Juan   Seoul   Singapore
Sydney   Toronto

Library of Congress Cataloging-in-Publication Data

Pring, Martin J.
    How to select stocks using technical analysis / by Martin J. Pring.
       p.   cm.
    ISBN 0-07-138404-9
    1. Investment analysis. 2. Stocks. 3. Stock price forecasting. I.
Title.

  HG4529 .P7465 2002
  332.63'2042—dc21   2002003899

McGraw-Hill

A Division of The McGraw·Hill Companies

1 2 3 4 5 6 7 8 9 0 AGM/AGM 0 8 7 6 5 4 3 2

p/n: 139855-4
part of ISBN: 0-07-138404-9

The sponsoring editor for this book was Stephen Isaacs and the production supervisor was Clare Stanley. It was set in New Baskerville by MacAllister Publishing Services, LLC.

Printed and bound by Quebecor/Martinsburg

This publication is designed to provide accurate and authoritative information in regard to the subject matter covered. It is sold with the understanding that neither the author nor the publisher is engaged in rendering legal, accounting, or other professional service. If legal advice or other expert assistance is required, the services of a competent professional person should be sought.

—From a Declaration of Principles jointly adopted
by a Committee of the American Bar
Association and a Committee of Publishers

McGraw-Hill books are available at special quantity discounts to use as premiums and sales promotions, or for use in corporate training programs. For more information, please write to the Director of Special Sales, Professional Publishing, McGraw-Hill, Two Penn Plaza, New York, NY 10121-2298. Or contact your local bookstore.

 This book is printed on recycled, acid-free paper containing a minimum of 50% recycled de-inked fiber.

To my favorite mother-in-law, Jimmie Sigsway

Contents

Acknowledgments

The year 2002 will see the publication of eight of my books by McGraw-Hill. Six of these form part of the Martin J. Pring on Technical Analysis Series, a series of multi-media CD-ROM/workbook tutorials. None of this would have been possible without the help of several key people.

In particular I would like to thank Jimmie Sigsway, my wonderful mother-in-law, whose support of our busy family allowed both me and my wife, Lisa, to allocated sufficient time to work on this project.

Without a doubt, a might thanks goes to Jeff Howard of Interactive Software Design, who has, as usual, pulled out all the stops and done a superb job creating the installation program and multimedia programming for the CD-ROM tutorial contained at the back of this book.

I would also like to thank many of our subscribers, workshop attendees, and purchasers of our CD-ROMs, whose kind and constructive comments have greatly encouraged me to expand the "Pring library."

Above all, a special thanks goes to my wife, Lisa, who, despite multiple pressures from major domestic construction work, minding the kids (including me), cooking the meals, and maintaining our Web site at pring.com, was still able to deliver the artwork for this book on time.

Preface

This book forms part of the series *Martin J. Pring on Technical Analysis*. Like all the others in the series, its main value lies in the CD-ROM enclosed in the back cover. This little disk contains a complete multi-media presentation of the subject matter contained in the workbook.

Years ago I published videos on technical analysis, but the CD_ROM format is far superior. Not only does each chapter play as a continuous presentation but also the need to fast forward or rewind is eliminated. Instead, the user can click on any subject matter in the contents and move instantly there. This format also allows for an interactive quiz, so the user can quickly move through multiple choice questions or chart examples, all of which are scored at the end. In this way, you can easily discover any area that needs brushing up. The only title in the series that does not contain a quiz is *How to Select Stocks Using Technical Analysis*.

The series itself is designed to expand on several of the subjects covered in the fourth edition of *Technical Analysis Explained*. Each of the book/CD-ROM combinations takes the reader into greater depth on the individual subjects. Diagrams and theoretical concepts are explained and then adapted to practical marketplace examples. It is normal in presentations of this nature to indicate the strong points of any indicator or concept, but these presentations also advise you of any known weaknesses of pitfalls they may have.

Technical analysis is the art of identifying trend reversals at a relatively early stage and riding on that trend until the weight of the evidence shows or proves that the trend has reversed. The objective of this series is to present a substantial amount of that evidence in the form of indicators and concepts, so that readers of the workbooks and viewers of the CD-ROMs will be in a stronger position to identify such trend reversals. Please take note of the fact that technical analysis deals in probabilities, *never* certainties. Armed with the information in this series, the probabilities should now move heavily in your favor.

With that in mind, good luck and good charting!

Martin J. Pring
Sarasota, Florida

How to Select Stocks Using Technical Analysis

Introduction

During the big bull market of the 1990s, most traders and investors found the process of stock selection to be very easy, especially in the technology sector. Tales of quick doubling, tripling, quadrupling, or more, of price, were commonplace in cocktail party chatter. The climate was not dissimilar to 1929, when bellhops and taxi drivers were available for instant investment advance, as if they had been in the business for years. More recently, the 1990 top in the Japanese market drew similar instant experts. Such stock parties are fun while they last, but once they are over, the hangover can last for many, many years. *A bull market is defined as an environment in which most stocks advance in price most of the time.* Normally, they last for one or two years, not for the unprecedented period of the 1990s. As a result, traders and investors got spoiled, and as the environment changed at the turn of the century, they ignored the stock selection process to their peril. Since reality has begun to set in, there has been a growing desire to learn more about techniques for selecting stocks. This book has been written to address these needs through the use of technical analysis.

Applying technical analysis to the stock selection process can be done in a number of different ways. Here, I will concentrate on what is commonly called the *top-down approach*. This will involve a little bit of elementary business cycle theory as it applies to the interrelationship of stocks, bonds, and commodities. The universe of stocks and mutual funds is huge, running into the tens of thousands. Consequently, it is an immense task to page through, or even scan for, such a huge quantity of stocks. The top-down approach attempts to accomplish this task in a systematic way. First, establish that the market itself is in a positive long-term trend, that is, a primary bull market. Then, examine the technical position of the 80 or so industry groups, then select several attractive ones. The final step is to zero in on the individual

1

stocks contained within that industry. One important question that needs to be answered when selecting any stock is that of time horizon. Are you an investor with a long-term, say, 9 months or more, timeframe? Are you more interested in playing the intermediate moves, that is, 6 weeks to 9 months? Or are you a short-term, 2–6-week, or even shorter, person? *The answer to this question has a great deal to do with the kind of indicators you might want to use.*

At the outset, there is one extremely important point that needs to be made. Whatever timeframe is used, it is mandatory to have a good understanding of direction of the main or primary trend. That is the bull or bear market lasting from 9 months to 2 years, or more. The reason for this is that *the direction of the primary trend dominates the magnitude of short-term moves and, therefore, affects the success or failure of your trading potential.* A rising tide lifts all boats, so it is safe to trade from the long side in a bull market. However, rallies in bear markets are very deceptive and are associated with far more whipsaws. It is, therefore, a wise policy to stand aside in a bear market, however bullish you may be over the short run. I will have a lot more to say on that subject later on.

Stock prices, like any other freely traded entity, move in trends. That is nice to know but would not have any significance whatsoever, were it not for the fact that trends, once underway, tend to perpetuate. The first part of this book will introduce several technical tools that will help in determining trend reversals at a relatively early stage.

Then it is possible to ride on the trend until the weight of the evidence, that is, the technical indicators, show or prove that the trend has reversed. To those new to the subject of technical analysis, a note of caution. The text assumes that you already have some basic technical knowledge of price patterns, trendlines, moving-average techniques, and so forth. If you sense a need for the basics, I refer you to my *Introduction to Technical Analysis*[1] or *Technical Analysis Explained*[2] book CD-ROM course.

A substantial part of this book will concentrate on the top-down approach and the group rotation cycle process, but I will spend some time on flagging some technical tools that can help in scanning huge databases of stocks. However, it is now time to begin, and our first part will describe the tools required to do the job. The first is the concept of "relative strength."

[1]McGraw-Hill, 1998
[2]McGraw-Hill, Fourth Edition, 2002

1
The Concept of Relative Strength

The Concept

Relative strength (RS) is a very important technical concept that measures the relationship between two securities. Incidentally, I will be using the term *security* throughout this book to include any freely traded entity, be it a market, stock, currency, commodity, and so forth. This way we avoid unnecessary repetition. It is important to note that relative strength, as we will be using it here, has nothing to do with Wells Wilder's relative strength indicator, or the *RSI,* as it is commonly called. The RSI is an indicator that measures a security's price relative to itself over a specific period. It is plotted as an oscillator and is a form of rate-of-change indicator.

Relative strength, as discussed here, is comparative relative strength, where one security is divided by another and the result is plotted as a continuous line. There are several ways in which relative strength can be used. The first approach uses RS to compare one asset to another, to decide which one to buy or to better understand an inter-market relationship. In this case, we might compare gold to bonds, to see whether the gold price is in a rising trend relative to bonds. If so, this could mean that an inflationary trend is unfolding.

Another possibility might arise when a review of the technical position indicates that both the U.S. and the Japanese stock markets are in a bullish trend. Analyzing the trend of RS between the two would show which market was likely to outperform the other.

In commodity trading, a *spread* is a form of relative strength. A spread involves the relationship between one commodity and another, such as corn to hogs. Alternately, a spread captures the relationship between a distant contract and a nearby one. In this instance, traders are attempting to discover relationships that have diverged from the norm and are riding on the spread until the two contracts come back into line.

A currency is really an RS relationship, when you think about it. For example, there is no such thing as the "U.S. dollar" in an external sense, because each currency is really a relationship between itself and other currencies. The dollar-euro cross, or the euro-yen cross, and so forth, represent other examples.

The most common use of RS is the relationship between a stock or industry group and the overall market, as measured by the S&P Composite, the NASDAQ, and so forth. When it is used in this way, RS becomes a very powerful concept for individual stock selection.

The RS Line

An RS line is obtained by dividing the price of one item by another. The numerator is usually a stock and the denominator a measurement of "the market" (for example, the NASDAQ or the S&P 500). The concept can also be expanded to the commodity area by comparing the price of an individual commodity, such as corn, to a commodity index, such as the Commodity Research Board (CRB) Composite, and so on. In Fig. 1-1 the price of the stock is featured in the upper panel and its RS in the lower one. When the line is rising, it means that it is outperforming the market. In this case, the denominator is the S&P Composite, so a rising line means that the stock is outperforming the S&P. Later on, it continues to rally, but the RS line peaks out. This means that it is now underperforming the market. Another possibility might involve the comparison of an individual country's stock or index to a global indicator, such as the Morgan Stanley World Stock Index. As long as the appropriate currency adjustments are made, the principles are the same.

The key thing about relative strength is that it moves in trends, just like the absolute price. This means that RS lends itself to trend-reversal techniques, such as price patterns, trendlines, and MA crossovers. The interpretation of trends in RS is subject to exactly the same principles as that of the price itself. It is important to note that an RS indicator is just what its name implies —relative. A rising line does not mean that an item, such as a stock, is advancing in price, but merely that it is outperforming the market or rising relative to it. For example, the market, as measured by the S&P

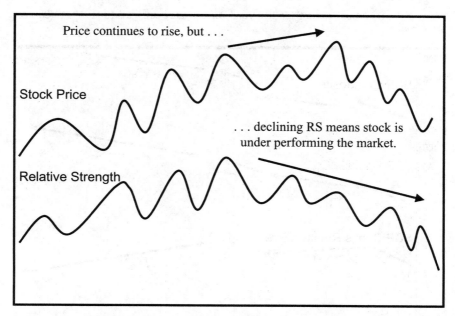

Figure 1-1 Price versus relative strength.

Composite, may have fallen by 20 percent and the stock by 10 percent. Both have lost value, but the RS line would be rising because the stock retreated less than the market.

Why Relative Strength Is Important

When we look at a chart of a rising price, we may say to ourselves that this is a good thing and that exposure to that security would have made sense. That is true as far as it goes, but if we watch the trend of relative strength, we can do even better.

Chart 1-1 shows the S&P Composite at the top and the S&P Banks in the middle panel for the period between 1941 and 1971. Everything looks pretty good because both series are in a rising trend until 1946 (arrow A). The RS line in the bottom panel is also in a positive trend, thereby indicating that the banks were outperforming the S&P, an ideal situation. Then, for the next 7 years or so (arrow B), the banks and S&P rise, but the RS line was trading more or less sideways. This horizontal trading action of the RS line

Chart 1-1   S&P Composite, S&P Banks and Banks relative strength, 1941–1971. (*Source: pring.com*)

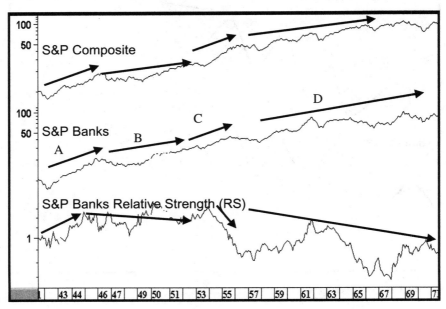

tells us that the bank's performance was on a par with that of the market as a whole.

In 1953 both the banks and the S&P begin what looks to be a nice rally (arrow C), but the RS line falls like a stone, clearly demonstrating that what looks good on the surface does not necessarily correspond to good relative performance. Finally, the rest of the chart, covered by arrow D, indicates that the satisfactory performance of the absolute price of the banking group was not telling the complete picture, since the relative line continued to underperform. In this situation, even though the banks would have made money, the declining trend of relative strength told us that there were other sectors where our capital could have earned a far greater return.

2

How to Interpret Relative Strength

There are various ways in which relative strength can be interpreted, but perhaps the most common are its positive and negative divergences, so let's begin with them.

Positive and Negative RS Divergences

When both the price and the RS are rising, they are said to be *in gear*. Important trends usually begin with both series acting in concert, but eventually the RS line fails to confirm new highs being set by the price itself (Fig. 2-1). This type of situation indicates that the odds favor the stock beginning a period of underperformance against the market. Weakness in RS, though, is not an absolute sell signal, that is, one indicating that the price will go down; it is merely a relative signal, that is, one implying a switch from an issue that has started to go out-of-favor to one that is coming into favor.

However, a divergence or series of divergences between the price and RS often provides an early warning sign of trouble, which is later confirmed by a trend-reversal signal in the price itself. Look at Fig. 2-1, for instance. The two are in gear at the start, but later on, the RS line diverges negatively with the price on three occasions. Finally, the price itself completes a top and declines. The top completion in this case confirmed the negative RS divergence.

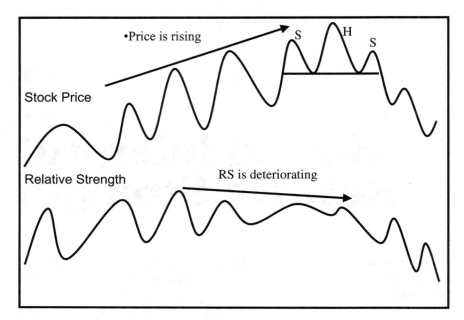

Figure 2-1   Relative strength negative divergence.

The opposite set of circumstances holds true in a declining market, in which an improvement in RS ahead of price is regarded as a positive sign (Fig. 2-2). Quite often, bear market lows in the equity market are preceded by an RS improvement in interest-sensitive stocks, such as utilities. This is because they are early leaders as a new bull market gets under way. This idea is discussed at greater length later.

Trend-Reversal Signals

Moving-Average Crossovers

Sometimes, it is a good idea to run a moving average through the price, using the crossovers as legitimate signals of a change in trend (Fig. 2-3). We can also do the same thing for the relative strength line. That is the theory. However, Fig. 2-4 is closer to reality because moving-average crossovers can prove to be extremely frustrating in practice, resulting in numerous whip-saws. In my experience, these whipsaws are even more prevalent with the RS line because it often contains a substantial amount of random noise. This

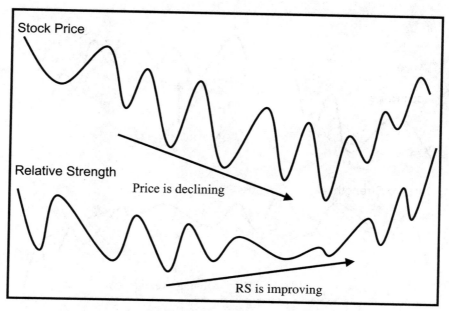

Stock Price

Relative Strength

Price is declining

RS is improving

Figure 2-2 Relative strength positive divergence.

is especially true for short-term trends, but even long-term moving averages, such as a 40-week or 65-week exponential, often result in misleading or whipsaw signals far more often than we might like. Chart 2-1 features General Electric. The RS line versus the S&P Composite is shown in the lower panel. GE is a relatively stable stock, but just look at the whipsaws generated from a 25-day MA crossover!

Now, if we extend the timeframe to weekly data (Chart 2-2), there are far fewer whipsaws. This time, I am featuring a 65-day EMA for both the price and the RS line. There is a concentration of whipsaws in 1994, but by and large, there are relatively few false signals in the 8-year history of the chart.

I mentioned that GE is a relatively stable stock. Now, if we turn our attention to another G-stock, this time GM (Chart 2-3), you can see that General Motors is far more volatile, even on this weekly chart. Once again, the two smoothings are 65-week EMAs. As you can see, the 1996–1998 period was particularly vicious.

Chart 2-4 just shows the *relative* action. This time, though, I have introduced an additional EMA. The dashed line is the 65-week EMA, but the solid one is a 10-week smoothing of the 65-week series. We are still left with a couple of whipsaws from their crossovers, but the 1996–1998 pounding of whipsaw signals is totally avoided, as the 65-week dashed line remains below the

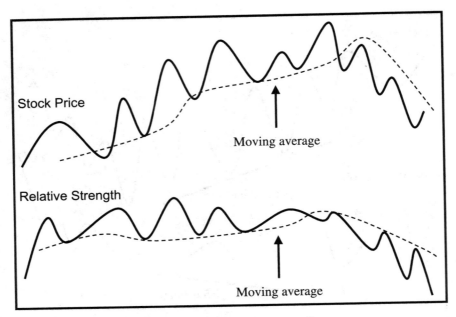

Figure 2-3   Relative strength and moving-average crossover theory.

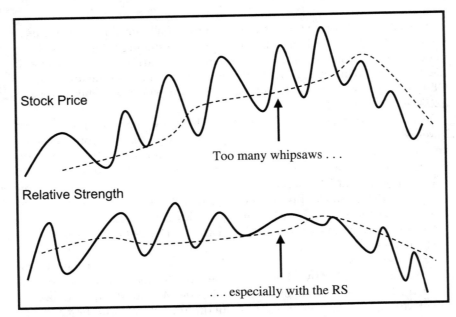

Figure 2-4   Relative strength and moving-average crossover reality.

Chart 2-1 General Electric, 2000–2001, and relative strength. (*Source: pring.com*)

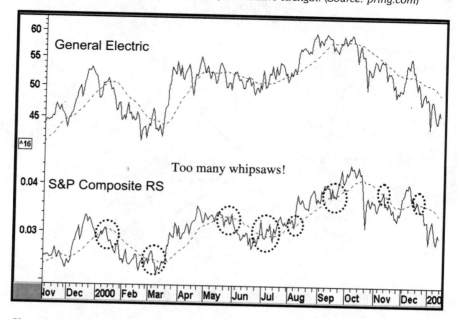

Chart 2-2 General Electric, 1993–2001, and relative strength. (*Source: pring.com*)

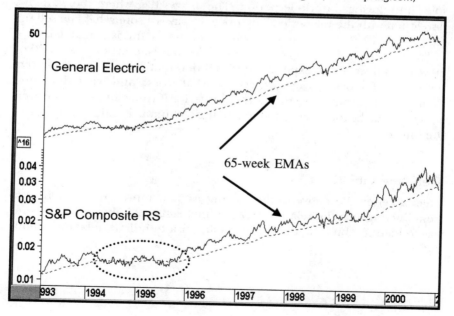

Chart 2-3   General Motors, 1993–2001, and relative strength. (*Source: pring.com*)

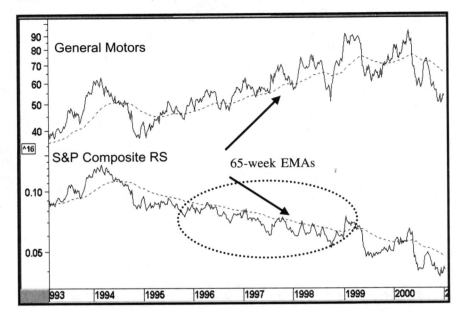

solid line during the whole period. The arrows flag where the whipsaws developed with the raw series. The price we pay is a somewhat late sell signal in early 1999, but in the total scheme of things, this is a small tab.

The best thing to do in any of these situations is to take a look at 10 or 20 years of history and experiment with different moving averages or combinations of moving averages, seeing what works and what does not. Remember to avoid curve fitting at all costs, for if you manipulate the averages to fit the historical data too much, the technique is unlikely to work in the future.

Trendline Violations

I feel a better alternative to the moving-average approach is to construct trendlines against the relative strength line. Figure 2-5 shows that a useful way to identify "buy" candidates is to wait for a trendline violation in both

Chart 2-4 General Motors relative strength line, 1993–2001. (*Source: pring.com*)

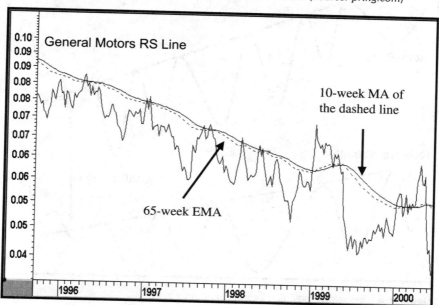

price and RS. The first thing to do is wait for a violation of the RS line. Then, when the price also confirms with a trend-reversal signal, you can take some action. These joint violations do not occur that often, but when they do, it usually signals an important reversal. Figure 2-6 shows another possibility, in which the bottom in the absolute price is preceded by a positive divergence. This is not a signal to buy, but it sets the scene for some positive action later on by indicating that the technical position is improving. This happens when the downtrend line for the RS line is penetrated, and this is later confirmed by a similar break in the absolute price. The confirmation does not have to be a trendline break, it could be a price pattern completion, a *reliable,* and I emphasize the word *reliable,* moving-average crossover, or even a rising peak and trough.

Figure 2-7 shows a similar joint penetration on the downside. In effect, these joint violations have the effect of reinforcing each other, which makes for a much stronger signal.

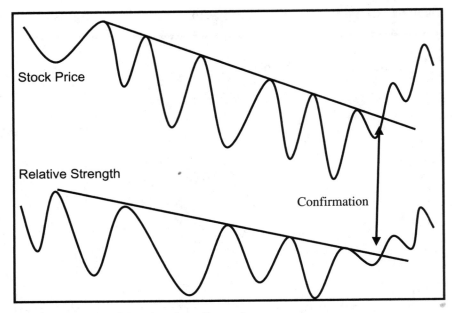

Figure 2-5   Relative strength and trendline analysis.

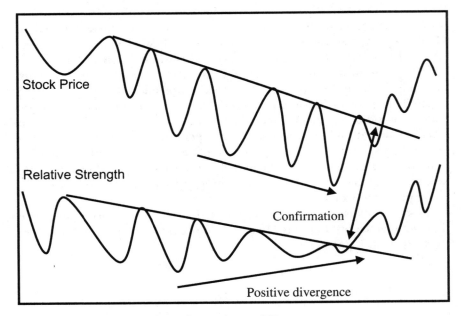

Figure 2-6   Relative strength trendline analysis and Divergences.

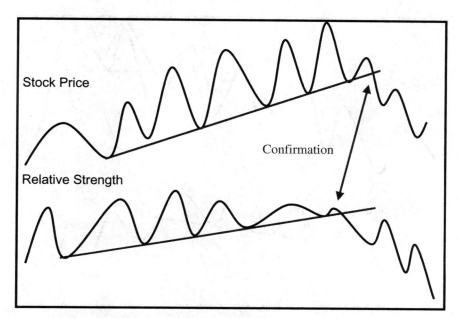

Figure 2-7   Relative strength and an uptrend line break.

Price Patterns

We can also employ price patterns when analyzing trends in relative strength. In Fig. 2-8 the RS line completes a head-and-shoulders top. This just tells us that the relative trend has reversed. This would certainly provide enough evidence to indicate that we should switch out of this issue in favor of one where the RS trend was reversing to the upside. However, if you want to make sure that the price itself is going to decline, as opposed to just underperforming, then a trend-reversal signal in the absolute price is also required. This would come on the violation of the short-term low flagged by the small horizontal trendline, since this would signal that the previous series of rising bottoms and tops had now been reversed with declining bottoms and tops. Note that even though the price subsequently rallies back through the line, this does nothing to reverse the peak-trough progression to the upside, so the trend is still regarded as negative.

Figure 2-9 shows the same type of approach, only this time involving a reversal from a downtrend to an uptrend. First, the RS line diverges positively with the price, our initial indication that both trends may be about to reverse. Then, the RS line traces out a rectangle and breaks to the upside.

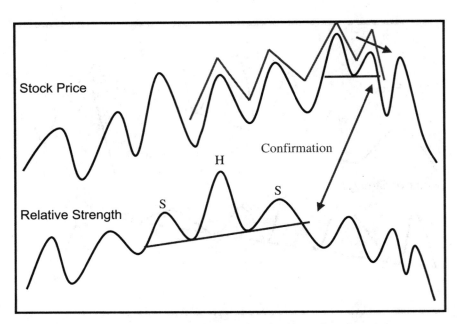

Figure 2-8 Relative strength, price patterns and peak-and-trough analysis.

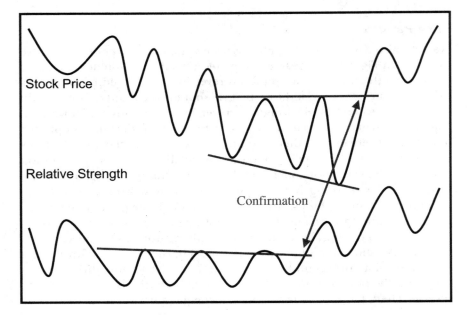

Figure 2-9 Relative strength and price patterns.

This is later followed by the price completing a broadening formation with a flat top. This acts as the confirmation signal that both price and relative performance have reversed.

The broadening part of the formation refers to the down-sloping line that approximately joins the series of declining bottoms. The flat top is the horizontal line. This formation is quite rare, but when it can be observed, it is usually followed by a very powerful rally relative to its size. It is really a reverse head and shoulders, where the price action is so bullish that the security is in too much of a hurry to trace out the right shoulder.

3
Marketplace Examples of Relative Strength

The S&P Oil and Computer Groups

Chart 3-1 features the S&P Domestic Oil relative strength line—relative, that is, to the S&P Composite. This is a very long-term chart that encompasses much of the twentieth century. It is useful, in that it demonstrates that the RS line lends itself to price pattern and trendline construction. These formations are not completed very often, but as we shall see, they are usually followed by a relative price move that lasts for many years. It is important to bear this in mind because most of the patterns I will be describing look small on the chart but extend over considerable periods of time. Their completion, therefore, signals a change in the environment that typically lasts for many years, even decades. For example, the line traces out a 15-year head-and-shoulders top in the late 1950s. A break of this magnitude signals a change in sentiment for a very long time. Indeed, it was not until the late 1960s that the RS line returned to the level of the breakdown point. A breakout from a reverse head and shoulders takes place in the 1960s, and the run-up in the 1970s and 1980s was signaled by a breakout from a double bottom. this was later reconfirmed by the completion of a consolidation triangle. In retrospect, the whole period containing the 1970s, 1980s, and early 1990s was one giant top. Anyone watching the break from this massive head-

and-shoulders top should have avoided this sector for many years. There was no way of knowing at the time that the RS line was going to experience such a long and precipitous decline, but the completion of the 20-year top should have been warning enough that the oils were not the place to be. Since this is a *relative* chart, it does not tell us anything about the *absolute* price performance of the group. Ironically, Chart 3-2 shows that the performance was positive. Even so, the decline in the RS line tells us that there were far more profitable places in which to invest than the oils.

The S&P computer—formerly office equipment—group is featured in Chart 3-3. It opens up with the violation of a 25-year uptrend line in the mid-1930s. This was followed by an 8-year consolidation. Later on, the RS line breaks above a 20-year downtrend line, and the breakout is followed by a long and very profitable ride. If you look carefully, you can see that the line was really the upper line of a symmetrical triangle. There was no way of knowing that this would be such a long and pervasive move at the time of the breakout. However, it could have been concluded with some degree of confidence that the computing group would outperform the S&P on a 5–10 year basis. After all, the violation of a 20-year trendline does not occur that often.

Chart 3-1 S&P Domestic Oil Index relative strength line, 1940–2001. (*Source: pring.com*)

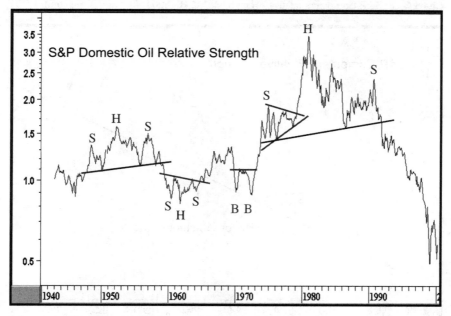

Chart 3-2 S&P Domestic Oil Index relative strength line, 1940–2001. (*Source: pring.com*)

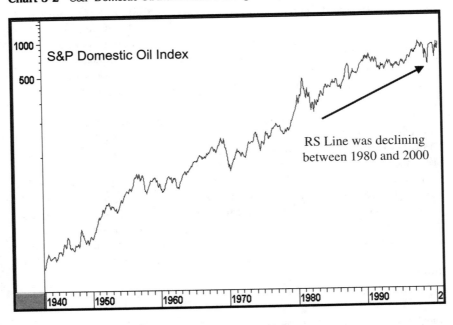

Chart 3-3 S&P Computers relative strength line, 1910–2001. (*Source: pring.com*)

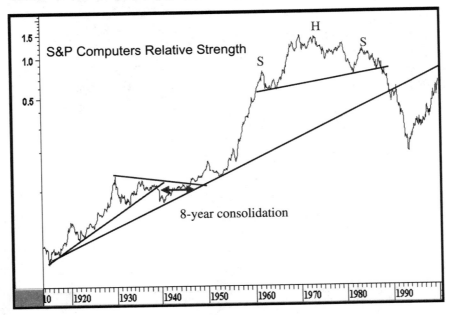

The next major event was the violation of a 30-year head-and-shoulders top in the late 1980s. This was followed by a dramatic decline. During the drop, this relative strength series also violated an 80-year uptrend line. Yes, that's right, an 80-year uptrend line. Even the superb rally in the 1990s only took the RS back to its extended twentieth-century uptrend line.

Obviously, we would not make a practice of studying these long-term charts every week or so, but, say, once a quarter, it does make sense to review the long-term picture of the relative-strength technical structure to see whether any major trends might be emerging. On a more regular basis, we would look at monthly charts covering a far shorter period of time, later moving down to the weekly and daily charts. I will be covering these short-term frames later, but for now, I would like to stay with the monthlies by examining a couple of individual stocks.

Individual Stocks and Relative-Strength Analysis

Chart 3-4 features Boise Cascade together with its RS line. Note that at the start of the chart, the RS line experiences a decline, whereas the price does not. I have called this a *divergence,* but technically it is not, because the price only comes close to its previous high. It does not exceed it. Even so, there is no mistaking the fact that the declining trend of RS is warning of trouble ahead. This is not confirmed, though, until we can construct a couple of uptrend lines: one for the price and one for the RS.

The RS trendline is violated first, and later on we get a break in the absolute trendline. This was then followed by a decline in both series. In this instance, initial weakness in the RS line was a warning of potential trouble in the absolute price.

Chart 3-5 shows that both series eventually bottomed and formed bases. In this instance, it was the price that broke out first. Normally, I prefer to see the RS take the lead, and its failure to do so raised a bit of a yellow flag. Just after the breakout, the absolute price rallies sharply and the RS eventually moves out from its base. However, the enthusiasm shown by the price is never fully supported by the RS line, which now starts to reverse to the downside. Everything is still okay at this point, because the RS is just experiencing a normal retracement following a breakout. The decline ends below the breakout point, and after a small rally, it becomes obvious that the low at point A is a crucial benchmark. If the line subsequently falls below point A, then this will indicate that a series of declining peaks and troughs is now in force. It will also signal that the RS breakout was a false one. Whipsaw breakouts are typically followed by a move in the opposite direction

Chart 3-4   Boise Cascade and a relative strength line, 1984–2000. (*Source: pring.com*)

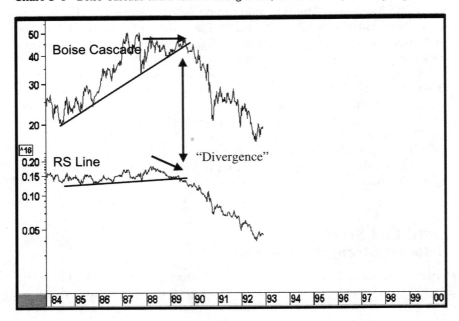

to that indicated by the breakout. The price itself establishes a bottom, and this, too, is a key benchmark, because its violation will result in a series of declining peaks and troughs. Chart 3-6 shows that the RS line gets into serious trouble as it violates its post-breakout low. In addition, the price itself breaks its previous bottom. This joint action provides us with the information to sell. Note that the RS line has now fallen to a new bear market low at this point.

As it turned out, the absolute price experienced a trading range with lots of misleading price action and did not decline until the very end of the chart. However, the persistent and continued drop in the RS line indicated that there were far better places to invest, since Boise was severely underperforming in the market throughout the whole period.

Looking for Whipsaws

When a joint breakout develops, it is reasonable to expect the trend to change, either to reverse or move sideways. However, we must always be on our guard for whipsaw signals because prices are determined by psychology, and we know for a fact that people can, and do, change their minds.

Chart 3-5 Boise Cascade and a relative strength line, 1984–2000. (*Source: pring.com*)

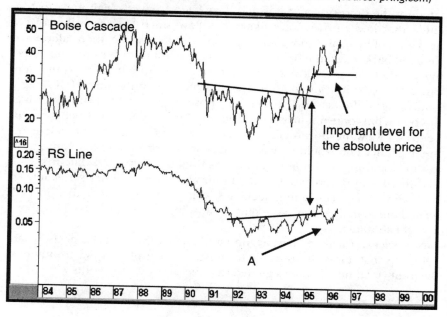

Chart 3-6 Boise Cascade and a relative strength line, 1984–2000. (*Source: pring.com*)

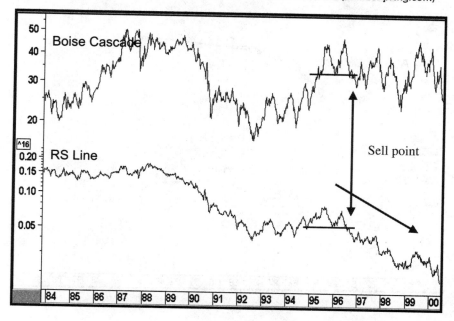

In this respect, Chart 3-7 features Alberto Culver. Two trendlines are violated on the downside and it would have been perfectly legitimate to conclude that lower prices were likely to follow, since both trendlines were necklines of head-and-shoulders tops: they did for a while, then rallied and then fell back to test the breakout low. The big test then became one of seeing whether the initial low would be taken out. Failure to do so would indicate a lack of downside follow-through, which is not the norm following a head-and-shoulders top. The technical position was certainly not bullish at this point, but some doubt as to the validity of the sell signal was being raised. Let us say we went short on the downside breakout, that is, the break below the neckline. This would now necessitate an exit strategy in our game plan, just in case things did not materialize as originally expected. The first clue that the downside breakout would be invalid arises if either series moved back above their respective necklines. Chart 3-8 shows that this, in fact, turned out to be the case. Note that the absolute price also moved up above its right shoulder.

Now we can turn the chart around and look at the bullish aspects. Chart 3-8 shows that it was also possible to construct a couple of downtrend lines, the joint violation of which signaled that the previous breakouts were whip-

Chart 3-7   Alberto Culver and a relative strength line, 1980–2000. (*Source: pring.com*)

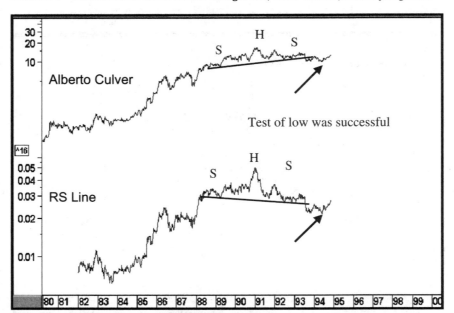

Chart 3-8 Alberto Culver and a relative strength line, 1980–2000. (*Source: pring.com*)

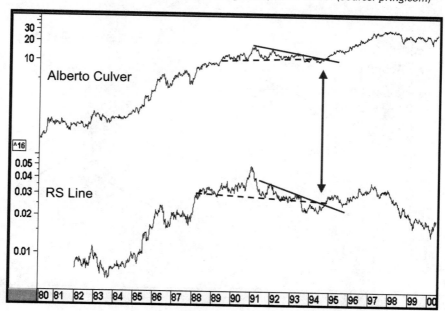

saws. Since whipsaws are usually followed by sharp movements in the opposite direction, the trendline breaks represented signals to actually go long. Also, both the absolute and relative prices had begun a series of rising peaks and troughs, thereby adding further weight to the bullish case. As you can see, this was followed by a very worthwhile move.

Keep an Open Mind

Our final example in this series comes from Abbott Labs in Chart 3-9. The chart shows that the RS line makes a new high, whereas the price does not, in April 1986. On the surface, this would appear to be a positive factor. However, positive divergences come after declines, not advances. If the price fails to confirm the RS line after a rally, this should be treated as a disagreement. Then, if both price and the RS line experience breakdowns of any kind, a sell signal is triggered. This is exactly what happened in this situation because both series violated important uptrend lines.

Later on, it was possible to construct another couple of trendlines that were both violated on the downside. Note how the break in the absolute

Chart 3-9 Abbott Labs and a relative strength line, 1985–1987. (*Source: pring.com*)

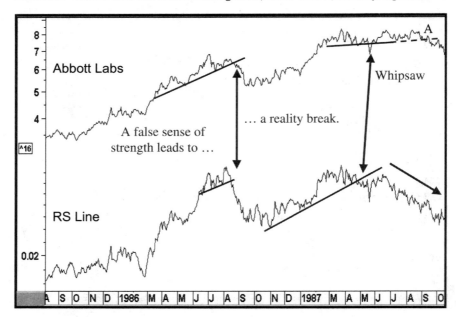

price turned out to be a whipsaw but that in the RS line was not. Whenever you see a weak RS line like this, it is time to get concerned. First, even if the price goes on to make a new high, the declining RS line indicates that there are better places to be invested. Second, the weakening RS is often a tip-off that the technical structure of the absolute price is not so hot. After all, if the price is going up at a slower pace than the market, should not this make it a strong candidate for a decline when the market itself reverses to the downside?

As we move to the right-hand part of the part, you can see what I mean. The price moves sideways, and the extended trendline is once again penetrated at point A. Also, the RS line is very weak and goes on to register a new bear market low.

In conclusion, it is pretty evident that the RS line can be a useful tool. First, by warning of the improving or deteriorating underlying technical strength or weakness in the absolute price. In other words, if RS is weakening while the price is rising, this is a bad sign, and vice versa. Second, RS trends in themselves help to point us to the strongest stocks or, alternately, the weaker ones that should be avoided.

Relative Strength and Short-Term Momentum

Trends in RS can also be analyzed from a momentum viewpoint. In Chart 3-10 of Abbott Labs, the relative price is in the top panel, followed by a 14-day RSI of the RS line and finally an MACD of the RS line. It is fairly evident that there are two main environments. First, a bear market develops between the end of 1998 and the start of the year 2000. This is then followed by a bull move. Now take a closer look at the MACD. During the bear market, it fails to reach an overbought condition, yet oversold readings fail to signal rallies. The opposite is true during the bull phase. This is typical of oscillator actions, which change their characteristics in primary bull markets. Just like birds in the northern hemisphere, oscillators migrate to the south during the winter or bear market, and to the north in the summer or bull market. *Whenever you can spot a situation where an oversold oscillator fails to trigger much in the way of a rally, this represents a tip that the prevailing trend may be bearish.* It does not happen every time, of course, but in many cases, this rule will work out.

Chart 3-10 Abbott Labs relative strength line and two indicators, 1998–2001. (*Source: pring.com*)

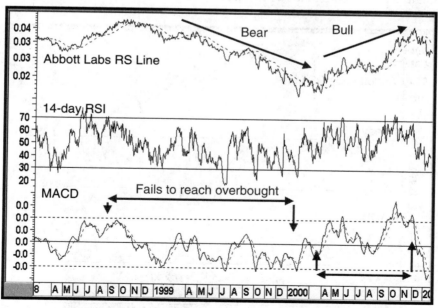

Now we can set about analyzing the RS trend. The actual top develops at the tail end of the arrow in Chart 3-11 at point A. Signs of weakness soon began to appear, as both the RSI of relative strength and the MACD of relative strength violated uptrend lines. This was then confirmed by the RS line itself violating an uptrend line. The joint action was not important enough to signal a bear market, but it definitely indicated that the uptrend would be stalled for several months. In effect, it would have told us that Abbott Labs was unlikely to outperform the market during the following months. As it turned out, the RSI trendline was the neckline of a head-and-shoulders top.

As 1999 unfolded, the price action became progressively more disappointing. The oversold condition at B merely triggered a sideways trading range, after which the relative downtrend is resumed. Also, consider the trendline breaks just after B. They should have been followed by a good rally, but they were not. When you see this type of action, it is usually a sign of a bear market. Indicators that give false signals are typically experiencing countertrend moves, and the real trend then develops in the opposite direction. Another set of trendline breaks proves to be disappointing just after point C. Chart 3-12 includes the same three indicators of relative strength,

Chart 3-11   Abbott Labs relative strength line and two indicators, 1998–2001. (*Source: pring.com*)

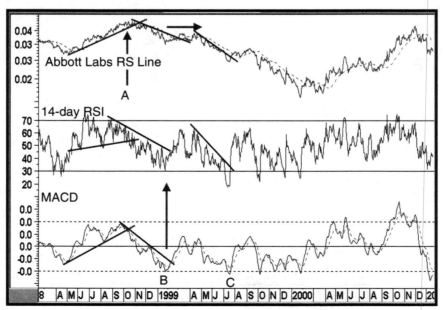

but this time I have included the actual price in the top panel. The arrow at A is the approximate point where the relative sell signal was triggered earlier. However, Chart 3-12 shows that the absolute price continued to extend its rally. It then diverged negatively with the RS line, indicating underlying technical weakness. However, it remained above the very significant September 1998/January 1999 uptrend line until the confirmation point in January 1999, where the trendline violation triggered a sell signal. If the sell signals in the RS line that had developed previously were not sufficient evidence to justify liquidation, the violation of this trendline in the absolute price certainly was.

Chart 3-13 shows the more bullish period featured partly in Chart 3-12. Remember, coming into this period the RS line had been in a strong bear market, in which the momentum indicators had been triggering false signals. However, at point A we see some positive action by both momentum series, since they barely fell below the equilibrium level at the time of the second low in the RS line in the top panel. Note also that the MACD had moved above its previous peaks, indicating a probable change in character more suitable for a bull than a bear market.

Chart 3-12 Abbott Labs relative strength line and two indicators, 1998–1999. (*Source: pring.com*)

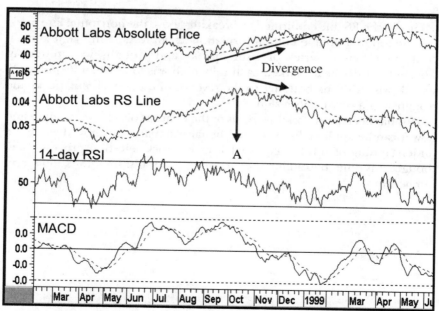

Chart 3-13 Abbott Labs relative strength line and two indicators, 1999–2000. (*Source: pring.com*)

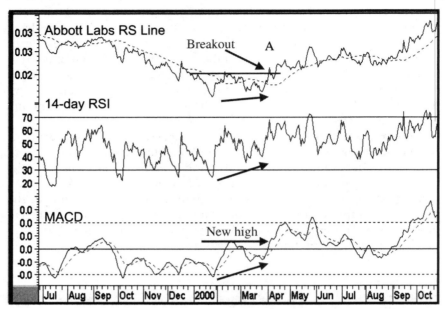

Finally, the RS line confirmed by breaking above the horizontal line marking the top of a double bottom formation at point A. At the same time, it confirmed that a series of rising peaks and troughs was underway. Throughout the bear market, each rally high was lower than its predecessor; likewise with the bottoms, so the reversal of these declining peaks and troughs was a very positive sign.

This has been a very brief synopsis of the concept of relative strength and how it can be applied, but it should be fairly apparent by now that a good understanding of this subject is vital in the stock selection process. Now, though, it is time to examine the second of our tools: smoothed long-term momentum.

4

Smoothed Long-Term Momentum

The Market Cycle Model

There are many trends in technical analysis, but the most widely followed are the short-, intermediate-, and long-term. The long-term is often referred to as a *primary bull or bear market*. It is represented in Fig. 4-1 by the thick line. Primary uptrends and downtrends typically last from as little as 9 months to as much as 3 years, or more. Because it takes longer to build than to tear down, a primary uptrend normally lasts longer than a downtrend. The time separating the lows approximates a little under 4 years. I will have a lot more to say on the primary trend later. But for now, I would like to leave you with the thought that the primary trend revolves around the so-called *4-year business cycle*. Also, it is important to try to gain an understanding of not only the *direction* of the main trend but its *maturity*, as well. *This is crucial for both investors and traders*. Obviously, if you are an investor with a 6-month–2-year time horizon, positioning yourself at the optimum time on the primary trend bell curve is self-evident. However, *traders with a 2–6-week time horizon should also be aware of the direction and maturity of the primary trend*. This is because a primary trend lifts or drops all boats and the magnitude and reliability of short-term trends are greatly influenced by the direction of the primary trend. I will have more to say on that one a little later.

Prices do not rise and fall in a straight line but are interrupted by intermediate rallies and reactions, as represented by the thin solid line. These intermediate moves normally last from as little as 6 weeks to as much as 9 months. In a bull market, rallies will generally last longer than in a bear

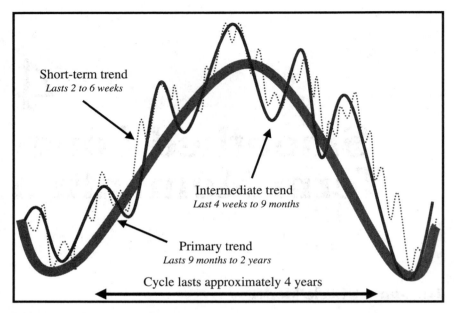

Short-term trend
Lasts 2 to 6 weeks

Intermediate trend
Last 4 weeks to 9 months

Primary trend
Lasts 9 months to 2 years

Cycle lasts approximately 4 years

Figure 4-1   The market cycle model.

market, and vice versa. In some instances, when they are contratrend moves, intermediate price movements can take as little as three weeks. Intermediate rallies and reactions are also interrupted, this time by short-term trends lasting from 2 to 6 weeks. Short-term trends are represented in Fig. 4-1 by the dotted line.

These are not the only trends in existence. For example, the secular trend lasts from 8 to 25 years and embraces many primary trends. By the same token, short-term trends can be broken down to even briefer periods plotted from hourly and other intraday data. For the purposes of this presentation, though, we will be concentrating on the short, intermediate, and primary trends.

When we are selecting stocks, it is very important to make an effort at determining the current position on the long-term cycle flagged by the thick solid line. I have some tools that will help us to accomplish this objective, but first we need to have a greater understanding of why the knowledge of the primary trend is important for both investors and short-term traders.

Why Knowledge of the Primary Trend Is Important for Both Investors and Short-Term Traders

The rising-tide-lifts-all-boats principle also applies to markets, in that short-term buy signals in a primary bull market usually result in a worthwhile move. Conversely, a sell signal in a bull market is often followed by a consolidation or no decline at all. The same principle applies in bear markets, but in reverse. For example, a sell signal will usually be followed by a worthwhile shorting opportunity, whereas buy signals more often than not will result in consolidations or whipsaws rather than a good tradable opportunity. In effect, and this is extremely important to understand, *if a whipsaw is going to arise, it will invariably develop in a contratrend way.* This means that if you are scanning your database for short-term buy candidates, you should always try to make sure that the stock you are monitoring is in a primary bull market. When looking for short candidates, try to establish that the stock in question is experiencing a primary bear market. It is not always possible to get an accurate fix, of course. But just the same, if the technical evidence strongly points to a bear market, however bullish the short-term picture might look, you should avoid buying. If a whipsaw signal is going to arise, the most likely place will be in a bear market.

Chart 4-1 has been divided into primary bull and bear markets. The solid bar at the top represents the bull moves and the dashed ones bear markets. The first two primary trends have been flagged with the arrows. You may have noticed that the price has been highlighted in gray and black lines. These differences are triggered by a short-term momentum signal. That signal takes place as the 14-day RSI crosses above and below its equilibrium line, that is, the 50-level. I am not recommending this system, merely using it as a device to trigger bullish and bearish short-term environments. The objective of the exercise is to make a point about short-term signals that develop in the direction of the main trend and those that develop in a contrary direction. In this respect, you can see that all the signals contained in the ellipses are whipsaws. Not only that, but they are also contratrend signals. The one on the extreme left, for example, is a bull signal in a bear market. The next one, in early 1992, is a sell signal in a bull market, and so forth. Generally speaking, then, the odds favor most pro–primary trend short-term signals being profitable, though we cannot say that this is always the case since *there is no such word as "always" when it comes to technical analysis.*

Chart 4-1 Hartford Steam and short-term buy and sell signals, 1998–2001. (*Source: pring.com*)

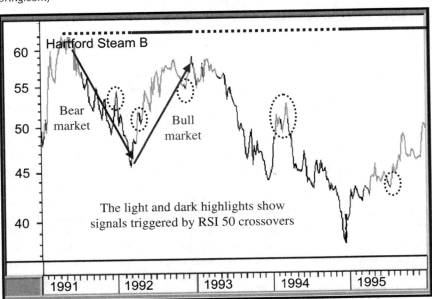

Chart 4-2 features German government bonds, known as *Bunds*. The principle is the same, in that the thick and thin highlights mark the primary trends, but this time, the triggering mechanism is a 10-week moving-average crossover. Just to show that not every short-term signal triggered in the direction of the main trend is profitable, I've highlighted some whipsaw signals in the two rectangles. The rectangle on the left is a consolidation pattern and both buy and sell signals result in whipsaws. There is nothing unusual in this because trading ranges do develop during primary up- or down-trends. Consequently, whipsaw buy signals do occur in primary bull markets, and vice versa. Even so, the signals in the ellipses also indicate that the majority of false signals do develop in a contratrend manner.

Long-Term Momentum

If we could quickly identify every primary trend reversal we would have it made. Unfortunately, it is not as simple as that. Often, the indicators we are using do not signal reversals until well after the fact. One useful method is to take a 12-month moving-average crossover as a signal of a primary trend

Chart 4-2 German Bunds and short-term buy and sell signals, 1998–2001. (*Source: pring.com*)

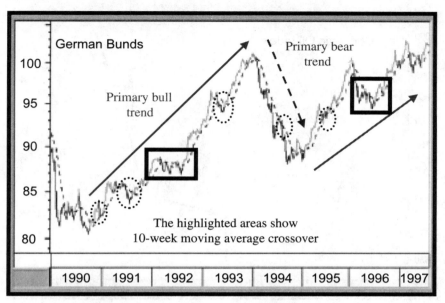

reversal. I took this timeframe because it has tested reasonably well over many markets. The 6- and 7-month periods have also tested quite well, though it should be noted that no timeframe is perfect and all leave a lot to be desired. In Chart 4-3 of the S&P Domestic Oil Index, you can see that there were some good signals, but there were also numerous whipsaws. Finally, we can also see that the early 1999 buy signal was unduly late. This is only one of a number of techniques for identifying long-term trend reversals. We may, for example, observe the completion of major price patterns, trendline violations, and so forth. None of them is perfect and not all, except for moving-average crossovers, are consistently present at these important juncture points.

One of the drawbacks of technical analysis that we need to come to terms with is that no indicator is perfect, so compromises are often necessary. One useful idea is to calculate a smoothed long-term momentum indicator as a way of replicating the primary-trend sine curve shown in Fig. 4-1. The advantage of a momentum indicator that has been smoothed, as opposed to one in its raw state, is that it traces a slow deliberate path and offers good perspective. Thus, it is far easier to judge whether the primary trend is oversold and likely to turn up, or overbought and, therefore, ready to move into

Chart 4-3   S&P Domestic Oil Index and 12-month moving-average crossovers, 1992–2000. (*Source: pring.com*)

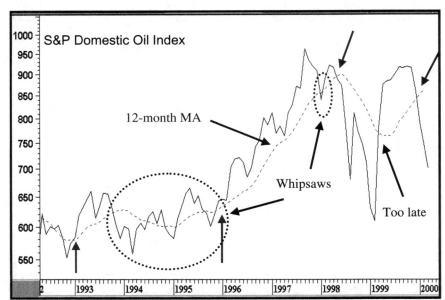

a bear phase. Momentum smoothings of this nature can be calculated and plotted for both the price and the relative strength line, but for now, I would like to concentrate on the price. The question is, What indicator should we use?

Stochastics

Chart 4-4 shows two smoothed momentum series for the S&P Aluminum Index. The objective is to try and come up with a series that reflects the major swings in the index and turns relatively closely to the primary peaks and troughs. The indicator in the center panel is a 36/15/9–stochastic. The 36 is a 36-period %K, the 15 is the slowing factor and appears on the chart as the black line. Finally, 9 represents the smoothing for the %D, which is plotted on the chart as the dashed line. There are many different ways of interpreting the stochastic, but in this presentation, I am just relying on the %K crossovers of the %D. As you can see, it does a reasonably good job of reflecting the broad swings in the index.

Chart 4-4   Alcan and two indicators, 1984–2000. (*Source: pring.com*)

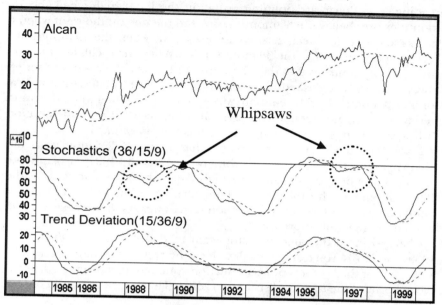

The problem is that we get a couple of whipsaws that are flagged by the two ellipses. This 36/15/9–combination is not the only possibility, but it was one of the best I could come up with. I show it merely because your software may not be able to plot some of the other indicators we are going to look at. While the stochastic is not a perfect indicator, we can say that it gets us into the ballpark from the point of view of identifying primary trend reversals.

Trend Division (Price Oscillators)

The series in the lower panel is a 15/36/9 trend-deviation indicator. A trend-deviation indicator is an oscillator or momentum series that is calculated by dividing a closing price or a moving average by a measure of trend. This measure of trend is usually a longer-term moving average. Chart 4-5 shows how it works. The top panel features the closing price and a 15-month MA. This moving average is also replicated in the middle panel along with a 36-month MA. The bottom panel is the trend-deviation indicator that is calculated by dividing the 36-month MA by the 15-month series. Whenever the two averages are at the same level, this shows up on the oscillator as a zero reading. The downward-pointing arrow on the left signals when the 15-month crosses below the 36-month series and the one on the right when it breaks above it. In effect, zero crossovers tell us when the 15-month MA crosses above and below the 36-month series. When the oscillator is in positive territory, it means that the 15-month MA is above the 36-month series, and vice versa. The dashed line plotted against the trend-deviation indicator is its 9-month MA. The 9-month MA is used for signaling when the trend deviation reverses direction. An alternative name for the trend-deviation indicator used in some charting packages is the *price oscillator*.

If you refer to Chart 4-6, you can see that the trend-deviation series did not experience the two stochastic whipsaws in 1988 and 1997. Also, in some instances, the deviation oscillator actually leads the stochastic, such as the 1985 bottom and the 1988 peak. Other turning points were more or less simultaneous. Thus the trend-deviation series appears to offer fewer whipsaws and is generally more timely.

Chart 4-7 shows the same indicator against the S&P Composite during the 1960s and 1970s. You can see that it reflects the cyclic waves of the S&P quite well. Most of the bottoms or accumulation zones are nicely signaled, as are the majority of the tops, or distribution zones. That sort of thing can be very

Chart 4-5   Alcan and a trend deviation indicator, 1984–2000. (*Source: pring.com*)

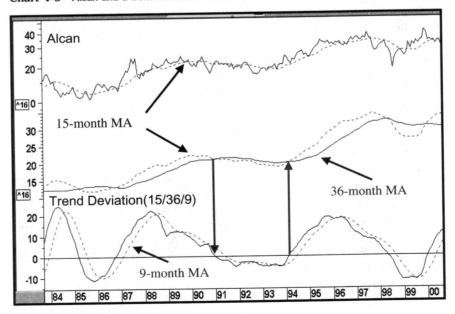

Chart 4-6 Alcan and two indicators, 1984–2000. (*Source: pring.com*)

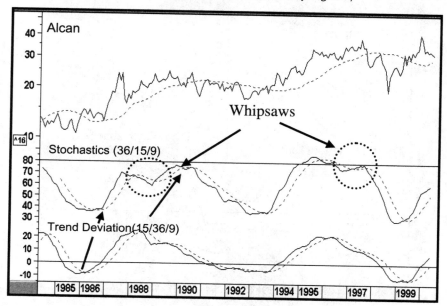

helpful for both traders and investors, alike. Investors have a relatively long time horizon and, therefore, find it useful to know when the primary trend for both the market and individual stocks is likely to reverse. Knowledge about the direction of the primary trend is also useful knowledge for traders, since short-term buy signals in a bull market have a tendency to be followed by the better rallies, and buy signals in bear markets by whipsaws.

It is important to note that while this indicator is reasonably consistent, it is far from perfect. Chart 4-8 features the S&P Financial Index. The turning points reflect the broad swings in the index, but some of the moving-average crossovers come too late to be of much practical use. The one in 1988, for instance, comes pretty close to the final peak, as does that in 1992.

A useful method of applying momentum is to make sure that the oscillator signal is confirmed by some kind of price trend signal. In the 1986–1992 period, no trendbreaks develop until the horizontal trendline is violated in late 1992. However, at that time the oscillator was quite overbought, which resulted in a high-risk signal. There is nothing in the book that says a signal that develops at an overbought condition will not be followed by an advance. However, the odds are much better if the crossover develops from close to, or below, the zero level. That is one of the reasons

Chart 4-7 S&P Composite and a trend deviation indicator, 1961–1981. (*Source: pring.com*)

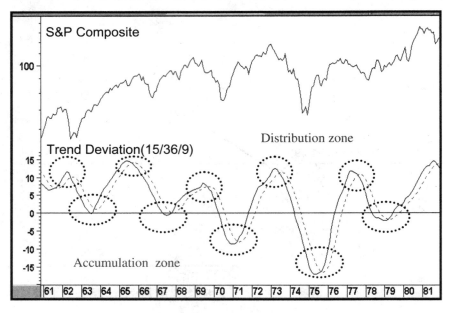

Chart 4-8 S&P Financial and a trend deviation indicator, 1983–2000. (*Source: pring.com*)

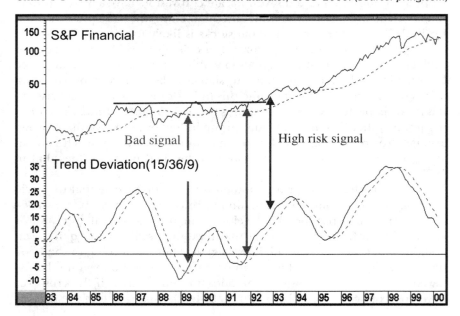

why *I prefer to use a guerilla approach to trading and investing.* In other words, to wait until several pieces of trend-reversing evidence are apparent and then act on that, rather than buying or selling on every signal without question. After all, if you went to the supermarket to buy some tomatoes, you would most certainly select the best, unbruised ones from the bin rather than taking the first ones that came along. The same should be true in markets. Only act on the better signals, where more indicators are pointing in the same direction and where oscillators are closer to oversold than overbought conditions.

One of the techniques we will be using later is to isolate an industry group, which looks good technically, subsequently examining the individual stocks in the group to see which ones look like good buy candidates.

Work Down from the Industry Group

Chart 4-9 features the S&P Aluminum group. By and large, the indicator exhibited deliberate swings, but there were two noticeable whipsaw signals in 1988 and 1992. One of the ways in which such misleading signals can be avoided is to wait for some kind of trend-reversal signal in the price itself.

Chart 4-9   S&P Aluminum and a trend deviation indicator, 1983–2000. (*Source: pring.com*)

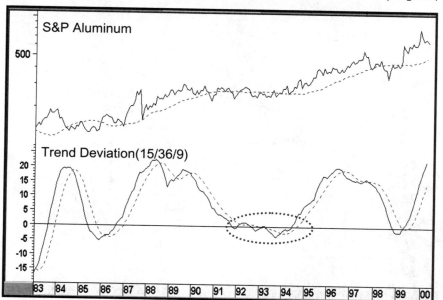

After all, you cannot buy and sell momentum, only price. All that the momentum is doing is indicating that the underlying technical position is deteriorating or improving. Only the price can tell us that it is responding to the momentum condition.

For example, in Chart 4-10 of Automatic Data, it was possible to construct an uptrend line between 1985 and 1987. When the line was violated, it confirmed the sell signal in the trend-deviation indicator as it crossed below its moving average. In the 8-year period between 1992 and the year 2000, there were three oscillator sell signals, none of which was followed by a decline. Indeed, throughout this whole period, the price fails to decisively penetrate its 12-month MA, represented by the dashed line. Even at the end of the year 2000, the price remained above its trendline. This is an extreme example, but it does demonstrate the importance of waiting for a price confirmation, however bullish or bearish the momentum indicator might look.

With that in mind, please refer to Chart 4-11, in particular the 1992–1994 period. You can see that the oscillator triggered two whipsaw signals. Note that the price never confirmed them because it failed to break to a new high. Later on it did, but first notice how it was possible to construct a small downtrend line for the oscillator. The third buy signal developed at around the same time as the trendline penetration, thereby offering a very strong

Chart 4-10 Automatic Data and a trend deviation indicator, 1985–2000. (*Source: pring.com*)

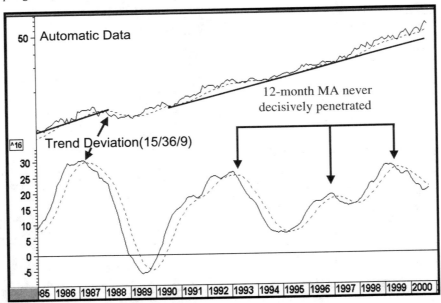

Chart 4-11 S&P Aluminum and a trend deviation indicator, 1987–1996. (*Source: pring.com*)

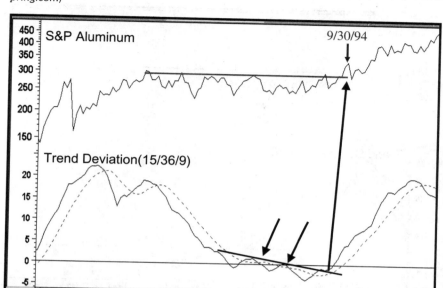

momentum signal. However, it was still only a momentum signal, and this was not confirmed until the price broke above the horizontal trendline on September 30.

Now let us look at some aluminum stocks to see. Alcan is featured in Chart 4-12. The technical action is very similar: the two whipsaws, followed by a trendline break in the oscillator, and finally a breakout by the price on September 30.

A very comparable picture was being painted by Alcoa (Chart 4-13), another stock in the group. This is because the same whipsaws and trend-break develop on September 30. However, Reynolds Metals in Chart 4-14 does not experience the September 30 breakout. It is true that the price broke above its high set earlier in 1994. However, it did not violate the trend-line. A violation did occur later, but the performance was quite disap-pointing. Some clues of potential weakness were given earlier. While the oscillator broke above its downtrend line at the same time it was crossing the MA, just like the other two stocks, it never experienced either of the whipsaws. In effect, it was weaker than the group index and the other two components. Also, the trendline for the price was horizontal for Alcan and Alcoa, but for Reynolds it was declining. All along, this was clearly the weak-

Chart 4-12 Alcan and a trend deviation indicator, 1987–1996. (*Source: pring.com*)

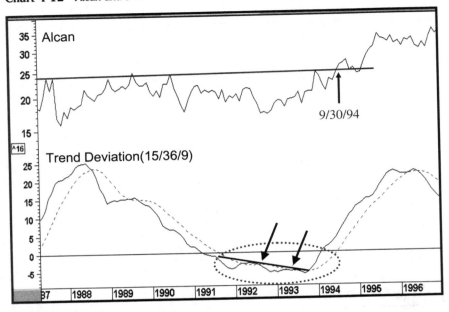

Chart 4-13 Alcoa and a trend deviation indicator, 1987–1996. (*Source: pring.com*)

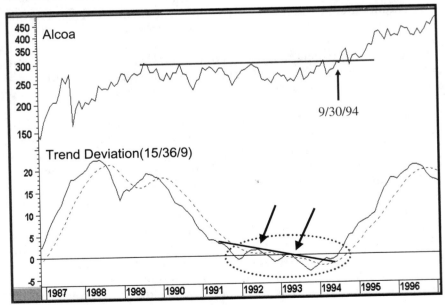

Chart 4-14 Reynolds Metals and a trend deviation indicator, 1987–1996. (*Source: pring.com*)

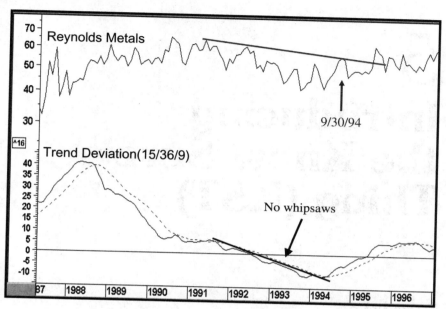

est of the three stocks. It demonstrates the rule that *in almost all cases of upside breakouts, it generally pays to go with the strongest stocks in the strongest groups.* Rarely does it pay to buy the laggards, because there is usually a good reason for the lagging action. In effect, strong groups and the leaders within the groups tend to get stronger. If the weaker ones do catch up, it is usually right at the end of the trend in which speculation is running rampant.

5
Introducing the Know Sure Thing (KST)

Introduction

It is fairly apparent that the trend-deviation indicator works reasonably well in terms of flagging the broad cyclical swings and registering relatively early turning points. However, there is an oscillator that I prefer to use, and that is the Know Sure Thing (KST). I developed this indicator many years ago *to obtain a good compromise between timeliness and sensitivity.* Normally, the advantage of a very timely indicator that turns close to the final peak and trough will be offset by numerous whipsaws. Alternately, an indicator that avoids whipsaws will usually reverse direction far too late to be of any practical use. How does the KST achieve this fine balance? Well, if you look at Chart 5-1, featuring the S&P Composite, you will see that there is a major turning point at the vertical line. Underneath the S&P are three rate-of-change indicators. I have smoothed the actual data with a 6-month moving average, so their underlying trends are emphasized. Let us take a closer look at the 1981 top. See how the S&P peaks at the point of the vertical line. However, it does not immediately decline but experiences a sideways trading range. The reason for this is that the three cycles reflected by the oscillators are doing different things. The 6-month is declining, the 9-month is moving sideways, and the 12-month is still rising. In effect, the bearish trend in the 9-month

Chart 5-1   S&P Composite and three indicators, 1979–1988. (*Source: pring.com*)

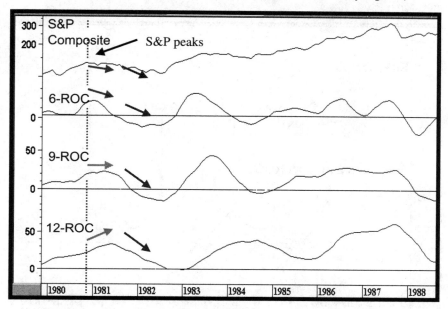

series is being offset with a rally in the 12-month indicator. Later on, at the second arrow, the S&P falls more sharply. Note that all three oscillators are now declining.

The technical principle we are dealing with here is that *price at any one time is determined by the interreaction of several time cycles.* In Chart 5-1, each ROC time span reflects a different time cycle. If all three series are reversing simultaneously, that means that at least three time cycles are doing the same, as well. Generally speaking, *the more cycles that are moving in the same direction, the stronger the trend.* This is known as the *principle of commonality.*

Chart 5-2 features another smoothed ROC. This time it has a 24-month time span and the smoothing factor is a 6-month MA. As you can see, it reflects the major or primary swings in the market. The arrows mark the peaks of this smoothed series; several of them line up quite well with peaks in the S&P Composite. Others, such as the 1984 and 1987 tops, are not at all well signaled. Chart 5-3 goes through the same exercise with the troughs. For the most part, these signals are more accurate, with the major exception of the 1987 low, which was signaled pretty well at the peak of the 1989 rally. Thus, it would be helpful if we could come up with an indicator that

Chart 5-2 S&P Composite and a smoothed rate of change, 1973–1991. (*Source: pring.com*)

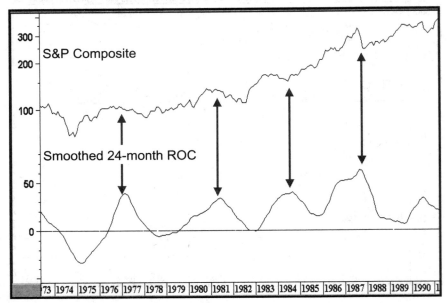

Chart 5-3 S&P Composite and a smoothed rate of change, 1973–1991. (*Source: pring.com*)

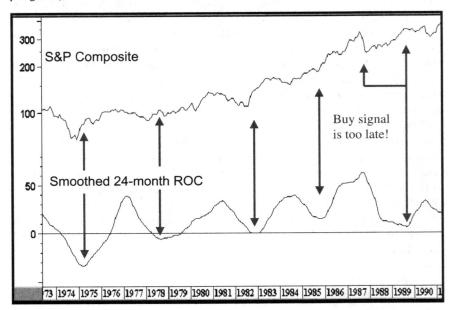

reflected all of the swings in the smoothed 24-month ROC. Yet it was, at the same time, more sensitive because it reversed direction closer to the turning points in the market.

That indicator is the KST.

Comparing the KST to Smoothed Long-Term Momentum

Chart 5-4 compares the smoothed 24-month ROC in the center panel and the KST in the lower one. It is fairly evident that the KST experiences all of the broad swings traced out by the smoothed ROC, but just as important, the turning points are more timely. The vertical arrows slice through the peaks of the smoothed ROC in the center panel. If you then look down to the KST, you can see that in almost all situations, it has already turned by the time it reaches the arrow. In other words, the KST retains the bull and bear swing characteristics of the smoothed ROC, but the important thing is that it reverses direction first. The 1984 peak was a failure with the smoothed ROC, but the KST catches it fairly close to the top. Only the lags

Chart 5-4 S&P Composite and a smoothed rate of change versus the long-term KST, 1979–1991. (*Source: pring.com*)

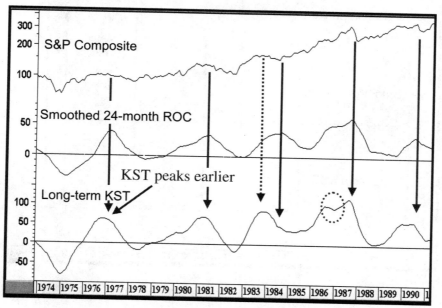

are different in each cycle. To be fair, I should point out that the KST did experience a small downturn in 1986, unlike the smoothed ROC. However, this is a small price to be paid for the superior signals elsewhere.

Chart 5-6 shows some arrows joining up the lows, and once again, the KST turns faster. This was especially true for the 1988 signal, where it changes direction well ahead of the ROC, which only turned in 1989. The KST did not bottom simultaneously with the market in October 1987, but no smoothed momentum series could be expected to do that. The important point is that it did start to turn, just as the rally started to accelerate to the upside.

The KST is normally plotted with a 9-month MA, where the crossovers are used as buy and sell momentum signals.

Table 5-1 shows how the indicator is calculated. There are four rate-of-change indicators with 9-, 12-, 18-, and 24-month time spans. The first three are smoothed with a 6-month MA and the 24-month with a 9-month MA. Each is given a weight, with the longest time receiving the greatest influence and the shortest the smallest. The whole thing is then added up and the result plotted as a KST.

Chart 5-5 S&P Composite and a smoothed rate of change versus the long-term KST, 1979–1991. (*Source: pring.com*)

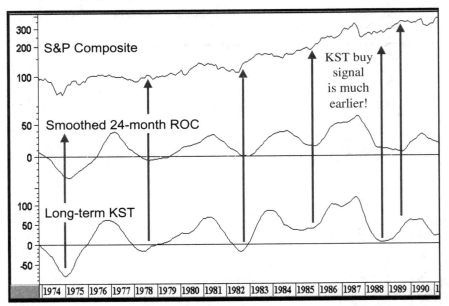

Table 5-1   The KST Calculation

Rate-of-Change	Smoothing Factor		Weight	Total
9-month	6	x	1	6
12-month	6	x	2	12
18-month	6	x	3	18
24-month	9	x	4	36
				72

This is a good, but *by no means perfect,* indicator. That is why I call it the *KST.* The letters KST stand for Know Sure Thing, because you know it is not a sure thing. However, it does provide a good framework from which to operate. The environment in which it does best is that where the stock or market revolves around the 4-year business cycle. Chart 5-6, featuring the S&P Composite in the 1960s and 1970s, offers a prime example. One caveat is that it does not perform during a very long-term or secular up- or down-trend, such as that shown for the Nikkei in Chart 5-7. The arrows in this instance point up several false signals. This again emphasizes a key point that *all momentum signals should be treated as alerts to buy and sell.* Serious action should only be taken when you can see that the price is responding by giving an actual buy or sell signal, such as a trendline break, moving-average crossover, and so on.

Chart 5-6 The S&P Composite and a long-term KST, 1963–1979. (*Source: pring.com*)

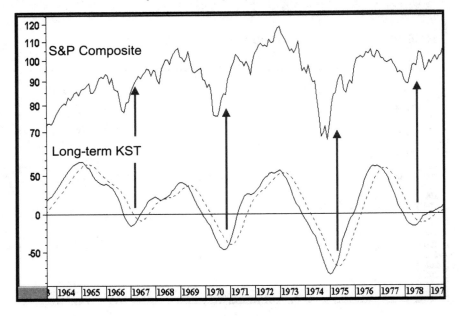

Chart 5-7 The Nikkei and a long-term KST, 1975–1992. (*Source: pring.com*)

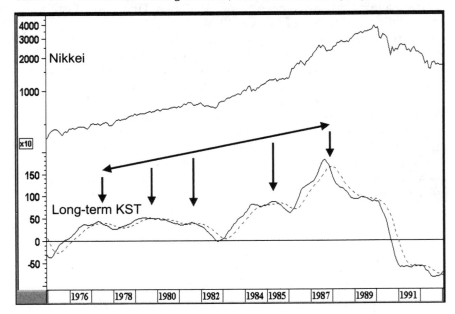

KSTs can also be calculated for intermediate trends using weekly data, short-term trends using daily data, and very short term trends using intra-day data. Their formulas are listed in Table 5-1. Later on, I will introduce some of these indicators, including KSTs calculated from relative-strength lines. Some of the formulas for these different timeframes are featured in Table 5-2.

Table 5.2   Suggested KST Formulas*

	ROC	MA	Weight	ROC	MA	Weight	ROC	MA	Weight	ROC	MA	Weight
Short-term[†]	10	10	1	15	10	2	20	10	3	30	15	4
Short-term[‡]	3[¶]	3	1	4	4[¶]	2	6	6[¶]	3	10	8[¶]	4
Intermediate-term[‡]	10	10	1	13	13	2	15	15	3	20	20	4
Intermediate-term[‡]	10	10[¶]	1	13	13[¶]	2	15	15[¶]	3	20	20[¶]	4
Long-term[§]	9	6	1	12	6	2	18	6	2	24	9	4
Long-term[§]	39	26[¶]	1	52	26[¶]	2	78	26[¶]	3	104	39[¶]	4

*It is possible to program all KST formulas into MetaStock and the Computrac Snap Module (see Resources, at the end of the book).
[†]Based on daily data.
[‡]Based on weekly data.
[§]Based on monthly data.
[¶]EMA

6
Financial Markets and the Business Cycle

The Cycle Follows an Orderly Sequence of Events

During the course of this book, we will have a lot to say about the group rotation process, since that has a tremendous amount of influence on selecting the right buying opportunities. However, before we get to that point, it is necessary to say a few things about the business cycle, since the prevailing stage of the cycle has a huge influence on the trend of interest rates, commodity prices, and the industry groups that are sensitive to such changes.

An examination of the economic indicators going back to the late 1940s, when economic data became more widely published, shows that the business cycle experiences a set series of chronological events. Just as the calendar year moves through the four seasons, so does the business cycle. This is invaluable information, for not only does it tell us that the cycle is not a random event but also that it has some order. If you know the current season in the calendar year, then you have a good idea of what to expect next. The same is true of the business cycle. If you can get an approximate fix on its current position, then it follows that you will have an inkling as to what type of conditions or events should be expected next. The exciting part is that turning points in the bond, stock, and commodity markets are part of this set sequence, and this can really help with stock selection. *Since the prices of many stocks are driven by changes in interest rates and commodities, you can appreciate that this linkage can really help in the stock selection process.*

There is another way to think of this concept. For example, if you are a gardener and it is obvious from the date that the current season is winter, it would be futile to plant seeds. Alternately, spring is generally the ideal time for planting. It works the same way with stock selection, because there are certain seasons in the business cycle when it is more profitable to invest in defensive stocks, such as utilities, and at others in commodity-driven equities, such as mines or energy.

The Business Cycle Sequence

The Commerce Department used to publish three important composite economic indexes every month: the Leading, Coincident, and Lagging Indexes. This information is now sponsored by the Conference Board, a nonprofit economic forecasting group. These indicators are expressed in Chart 6-1 in the form of KST oscillators. The very titles of these indexes should give you clues as to what they are measuring: leading, coincident, and lagging parts of the economy. When we talk of the economy growing or contracting, we think of the whole economy expanding or shrinking, but nothing could be further from the truth. In actual fact, *the economy consists of many different sectors that often move in different directions.* Some move ahead of the rest and are called the *leading* sectors. They include housing, consumer good orders, and so on. Coincident indicators apply to sectors such as capacity utilization, industrial production that roughly *coincide* with the middle parts of the economy. Finally, *lagging* sectors of the economy embrace capital intensive areas, such as basic industries capital expenditures, mining, and so forth. Thus, *the "economy" is really an aggregate term that describes a collection of individual cycles, all of which are in a different stage of development at any one point in time.* I often think of a person standing on the platform of a station. Instead of a long, straight track connecting it to other stations, this railroad track is circular. The journey taken by the train then becomes a continuous circle. Experience tells us that the train is arranged in a preset order. The engine is at the front, followed by the first-class carriages, and then the restaurant car. Then come the tourist carriages and finally the caboose holding up the rear. Anyone standing on the platform knows that once the engine has passed, they should expect the first-class section, and so forth. Once the caboose has passed, it is time to expect a new cycle in the form of the reappearance of the engine. The economy is similar, in that it undergoes a set series of chronological sequences. The engine that starts the whole thing off is an injection of liquidity or cash into the system. This occurs when the economy is in recession and is reflected in lower interest rates that encourage people to buy big ticket items, such as houses. Houses have to be furnished, and the next stage involves the manufacture and sale of these goods, and so forth down the line. The difference between the economy and the train is that the leads and lags for each economic event vary from cycle to cycle. Furthermore, these economic events occasionally develop out of sequence. This compares to the carriages on the train that are always a standard size and, unless someone makes a mistake, will appear in the same order.

Chart 6-1 shows this process in action. The arrows join the peaks and troughs of the smoothed momentum indicators. As you can see, they clearly translate to the right. The first component to peak is the Leading Index, followed by the coincident series. Finally, the Lagging Index is in the rear. This same chronological sequence is also apparent in Chart 6-2, which covers the end of the twentieth century. You may have noticed that the sequence for the last series of troughs did not work very well. This is because the Lagging Index in the bottom panel led the coincident series. It underscores

Chart 6-1   Leading, coincident, and lagging indicator momentum, 1965–1989 S&P. (*Source: pring.com*)

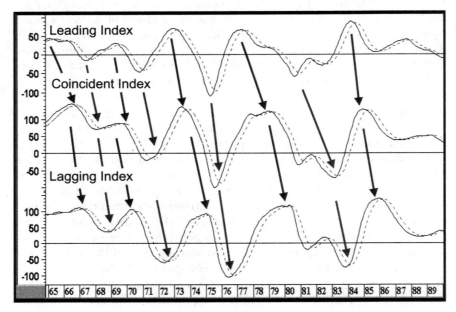

the point made earlier that not all sequences develop as expected and that the leads, lags, and magnitude of the swings vary from cycle to cycle.

This is more apparent when we expand on the number of displayed indicators in Chart 6-3. This one starts off with M2, adjusted for commodity prices, at the top. It is then followed by inverted short-term interest rates, housing starts, commodities, and, finally, our old friend the Lagging Index. The real M2 and the inverted short-term rates are financial indicators. They show that a prerequisite of any business cycle expansion is an increase in real money and a rise in the prices (decline in yields) of money market instruments. Housing starts are extremely sensitive to interest rates and are the first sector of the real, as opposed to the financial, economy to recover during an economic expansion. As the expansion takes hold, so the other sectors recover. Once again, it is possible to connect the troughs that usually translate to the right. The peaks are also connected. It is interesting to note that commercial paper yield topped out ahead of the real money supply in the early 1960s. This demonstrates that while this out-of-sequence behavior does not normally happen, it is certainly not unprecedented. In this instance, it is possible to construct an arrow joining M2 to housing starts. It then becomes apparent that with the exception of rates, the sequence is

Chart 6-2 Leading, coincident, and lagging indicator momentum, 1969–2001 S&P. (*Source: pring.com*)

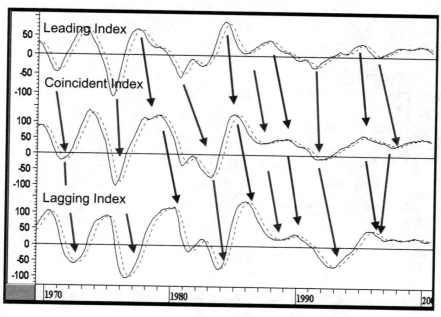

still in force. This out-of-sequence pattern tends to develop as we place more and more indicators on the chart. However, this is not an overwhelming problem because the position of the other series can be used as a cross-check.

If you look at the other arrows, though, you will see that all the other peaks and troughs were in gear. I do not wish to leave you with the impression that all periods are this easy to follow. Some, such as the late 1990s, were not. But by and large, this arrangement does show that the business cycle does experience a chronological sequence. It is, of course, possible to introduce many more indicators into the diagram, but this would make it far too complicated to follow. Using as many as five is bad enough.

The two main points to grasp at this juncture are:

1. *There is an order to the business cycle that takes the form of a chronological sequence of events.*

2. *As different economic sectors expand and contract, they affect the profit and, therefore, price performance of specific industry groups.* In effect, the orderly progression of the business cycle causes the rotation of industry groups to develop in the stock market.

Chart 6-3   Financial and economic indicator momentum, 1960–1972. (*Source: pring.com*)

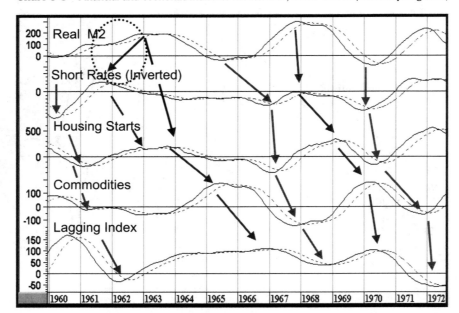

The Financial Markets and the Business Cycle

Figure 6-1 shows a sine curve that represents the growth path of the economy. You may be saying to yourself that we know by now that the economy is not homogeneous but consists of multiple sectors. So what is this curve shown here? The answer is that the curve is a proxy for the coincident indicators in the economy. Thus, parts of the economy are moving ahead of our curve, and other parts will lag behind it.

The horizontal line reflects the equilibrium level, where there is neither growth nor contraction. As the curve rallies above the equilibrium point, it means that the economy is expanding at a faster and faster pace, until it peaks out. At this point (A), the economy is growing at its fastest pace and the curve begins its descent. The economy still continues to grow, but at a slower and slower pace, that is, until it falls back to the equilibrium level, where there is neither growth nor contraction.

Then it falls below equilibrium, where business activity actually starts to contract. As the curve moves deeper below the equilibrium line, business activity declines at a faster and faster pace. As it bottoms (B), the pace of economic contraction is at its steepest. Then the curve starts to rally again.

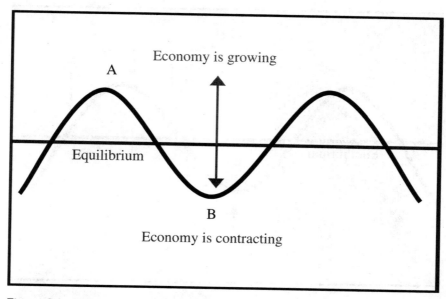

Figure 6-1 The idealized business cycle.

Activity is still contracting, but at a slower and slower pace, until it crosses the equilibrium level and a new expansion is borne.

Now it is time to use this business cycle diagram and our knowledge of the chronological sequences described earlier to explain two important concepts. First, how the three markets, bonds, stocks, and commodities, fit into this sequence. Second, we will build on this knowledge to better understand the group rotation process, eventually working down to our ultimate goal, the optimum selection of individual stocks.

A review of the last 200 years of financial market history—yes, you heard correctly, 200 years—indicates that in the vast majority of cases there is a definite chronological sequence of events that takes place during the course of the business cycle as far as the major turning points in bonds, stocks, and commodities are concerned. This progression consists of a bottoming-out in bond prices (peak in interest rates), then in equities, and finally in commodities. It continues with the peaking-out of bond prices (interest rates troughing), then stocks, and finally commodity prices. This idealized sequence is shown in Fig. 6-2. History shows that while this has been a fairly consistent relationship, there have definitely been exceptions to this chronological sequence. For example, in 1929, commodities peaked ahead of bonds. In 1989, the *top* in rates led the *peak* in equities, and so forth.

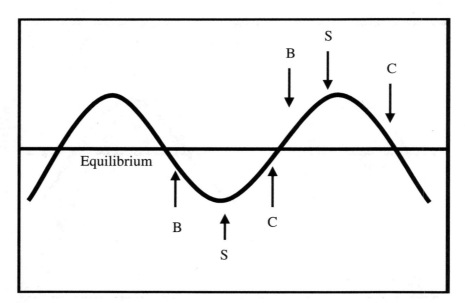

Figure 6-2 Idealized peaks and troughs of the financial markets.

Generally speaking, though, these out-of-sequence progressions are very much more the exception rather than the rule.

There are two variables to this. First, the magnitude of the individual bull and bear markets for bonds, stocks, and commodities varies from cycle to cycle. Second, the leads and lags between the peaks and troughs also differ. Chart 6-4 compares money market prices (inverted short-term interest rates) to the S&P Composite. I am using money market prices as a substitute for bonds, since they actually have a stronger and more direct influence on stock prices. In 1966, the two bottomed more or less simultaneously. In 1969, there is quite a long lead time between the top in money market prices and that in stocks, about 1.5 years, in fact.

In Chart 6-5 the lead at the 1980 top was only a few months, but two bottoms were separated by almost a year. Generally speaking, the longer the lead between money market and stock prices at a bottom, the stronger the equity rally is likely to be. That is because the failure of stocks to respond indicates a long and deep recession. During that period, corporations rush to cut costs and lower breakevens. Then, when the new recovery gets underway, the multiple effect on profits is tremendously positive, and equities respond accordingly.

Chart 6-4 Money market prices versus the S&P Composite, 1965–1977. (*Source: pring.com*)

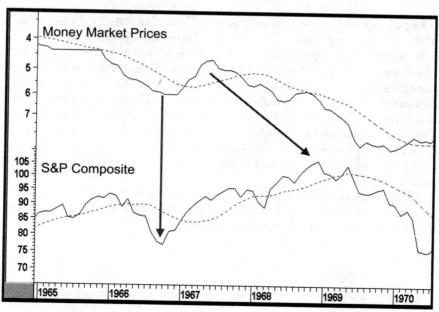

Chart 6-5 Money market prices versus the S&P Composite, 1971–1989. (*Source: pring.com*)

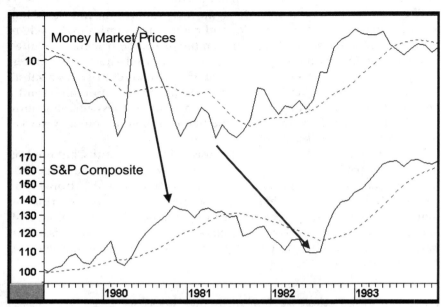

Knowledge of this rotation principle and the ability to obtain some kind of fix, however approximate, on the prevailing stage of the business cycle, have tremendous significance for the stock selection process, especially where the individual stocks and groups have demonstrated sensitivity to changing business cycle environments. For example, if we have a clear idea that the economy is in a recession, then it is normally safe to buy bonds and bond-type equities, such as electric utilities. This is especially true if it has also been established that stocks and commodities are in a bear market. In effect, *this progression of financial market turning points provides us with the basis for a framework or map, which can be used to formulate a more effective investment strategy.*

These relationships and their implications will be examined in subsequent sections, but first let us look at how and why this sequence occurs and how the business cycle influences market activity.

7

The Chronology of Bond, Stock, and Commodity Turning Points

Introduction

The chronological sequence of how bonds, stocks, and commodities revolve around the business cycle is shown in Fig. 7-1. A brief description of each financial market turning point now follows.

Interest Rates Peak

The cycle begins as bond prices bottom out and interest rates peak. An interest rate is the price of credit and, like any other price, is determined by the interaction between supply and demand. A fundamental shift in this supply balance has to materialize before interest rates reverse their upward trend. This almost always occurs *after* the economy has entered a recessionary phase.

Demand for Credit Declines

Recessionary conditions reduce the demand for credit, as businesses and consumers retrench. Loan demand normally peaks 2 to 3 months into the recession. It would be reasonable to expect credit growth to crest as soon

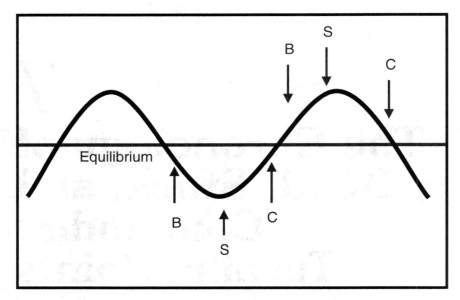

Figure 7-1   Idealized peaks and troughs of the financial markets.

as the economy begins to contract. However, this is not normally the case, because corporations usually find themselves in a cash squeeze at this stage in the cycle. Figure 7-2 shows how this works. During the recovery, sales (the dashed line) continue to expand. To keep up with this pace, inventories (shown by the stepped solid line) also increase. Then, at some point (A), sales start to slip sharply. Businesses immediately respond by not ordering any more inventory, but since sales are falling, they are stuck with a surplus. A cash-flow deficit results because revenues are not coming in fast enough to finance inventories. The deficit is made up through short-term borrowing. This effectively means a temporary scramble by many corporations, which are forced to borrow at virtually any price. This is one of the reasons why interest rates typically experience a parabolic rise at the end of the cycle. This process, known as *involuntary inventory accumulation,* usually lasts for about six weeks. It is almost like a corporate margin call. Whenever there are widespread margin calls, prices move dramatically, and this corporate margin call is one of the principal reasons why interest rate peaks typically end in a spike.

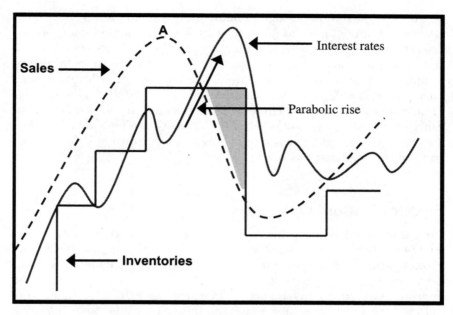

Figure 7-2   The involuntary inventory accumulation phase.

The Money Supply Increases

The Federal Reserve is a key player on the supply side. The Central Bank is engaged in a continual battle as it alternatively fights inflation or recession. When it becomes increasingly evident that the economy is in serious trouble, the Fed reverses its role as inflation fighter and takes on the unemployment battle. In effect, this results in a reversal from tight to easy monetary policy. It usually moves with a lag because it takes some time before all the economic numbers are reported and digested. Also, the Central Bank does not reverse policy very often. Thus, when the switch is made, the authorities are careful to ascertain that they do not give the impression of indecisiveness by subsequently reversing themselves.

As soon as the Fed realizes that recession is a serious problem, it starts to inject liquidity (cash) into the system through the purchase of Treasury Bills (known as *open market operations*). This, along with other measures, such as reducing the reserve requirements in the banking system, has the effect of increasing the supply of credit. The increased credit availability makes possible a decline in the federal funds rate and later the discount rate. It is important to note that *the Fed can directly control the trend of short-term interest rates* over the near-term through its influence on the supply side. It can only affect yields at the long end *indirectly* because that is the prerogative of the market itself. If participants feel that monetary policy is too easy and will later result in inflationary conditions, bond yields will remain high relative to short-term rates, and vice versa. In effect, if short rates fall against long rates, investors will extend the maturities of their portfolios. That much is within the power of the Fed. However, if investors feel that the risk of a resurgence of inflationary pressures and lower bond prices is high, they will forgo the (relatively) tempting prospects of longer-term maturities in favor of the safety of shorter-dated securities.

Equities Bottom Out

Once interest rates have peaked (bond prices bottomed), it is only a matter of time before equities also experience a low. This occurs when stock market participants conclude that rates have fallen sufficiently for a recovery to take place. Equities are then accumulated in anticipation of the upswing. If the recession has been particularly severe, it means that corporations have been more aggressive in cutting costs and lowering their breakeven levels. As a consequence, the rebound in stock prices is normally much greater, and the initial rally in the equity market can be explosive.

One clue as to whether the initial rally will be above or below average can be gleaned from the lag between the low in bond prices and that of stocks. Generally speaking, the longer the lag, the greater is the implied severity and duration of the recession. In 1877, for example, the lag was four years, and was followed by a doubling of stock prices. In 1920 and 1982, the bottom in bonds and stocks was separated by about a year, and both periods were associated with a longer-than-average bull market in equities.

One extremely important point is that *it is a prerequisite for a major stock market bottom to be associated with bad news*. In this case, a major bottom is defined as one that develops after at least a 1-year decline. By way of illustrating this point, Chart 7-1 compares the S&P Composite to a trend-deviation measure of the coincident indicators. The arrows intersect the stock market bottoms between 1957 and 1975. It is fairly evident that bottoms in the equity market developed pretty closely to the period of maximum economic contraction. The two lows in 1962 and 1966 (flagged by the dashed arrows) were not associated with a recession and followed declines lasting less than a year. Chart 7-2 shows the same arrangement for the balance of the twentieth century. The three solid arrows were each associated with recessions. However, the balance of the lows between 1982 and the year 2000 did not develop under the environment of an economic contraction, and the declines preceding them did not last for a year. The 1984 bottom was associated with a double-cycle growth recession,[1] 1987 was a severe technical correction unrelated to the business cycle, and the late 1994 low was again a growth recession double-cycle bottom. Notice that none of the declines in the 1990s were very severe, but that is not surprising because the economy from 1990 did not experience a recession.

Commodities Bottom Out

Returning to our business cycle model of the three markets, bonds and stocks are now both rising, but commodities are still experiencing a bear market. It is not until the recovery has been underway for a few months that they also reach their final low. Typically, the commodity markets bottom after the sine curve has crossed above the recession/expansion line. Occasionally, the actual price low occurs during the terminal phase of the recession, but even so, commodities usually remain in a wide trading range and only

Chart 7-1 The S&P Composite versus a trend deviation indicator of the coincident indicators, 1956–1980. (*Source: pring.com*)

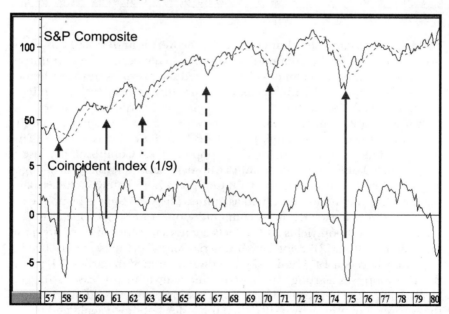

[1]This term is discussed later in the chapter under "Double Cycle."

Chart 7-2 The S&P Composite versus a trend deviation indicator of the coincident indicators, 1978–2000. (*Source: pring.com*)

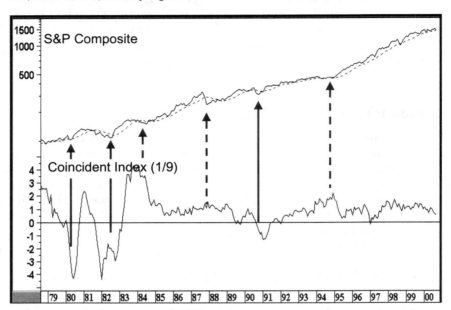

embark on a sustainable advance once the recovery is underway. Early recessionary bottoms in the commodity markets usually occur when an unusually large commodity boom has characterized the previous recovery. Under such circumstances, the final peak in commodity prices develops under a cloud of speculative froth, as both individuals and corporations attempt to cash in on the boom. An example is shown in Chart 7-3. The commodity series that is used in this book is the CRB Spot Raw Material Index. This series has been favored over the more popular CRB Composite because it is constructed only from commodities whose demand is sensitive to changes in business cycle conditions. The CRB Composite, alternately, includes many weather-driven commodities, such as grains. The CRB Spot is by no means perfect because it excludes a key commodity, oil. However, it appears to correlate well with bond yields and reflects changes in economic activity quite satisfactorily. The CRB Spot Raw Industrial Material Index experienced a huge rally between 1971 and 1974 and then bottomed in early 1974, just as the recession was starting. Weak economic activity in this case is flagged by the coincident indicator momentum crossing below zero. It was not until the recovery got underway in 1975 that the index bottomed again and began a slow ascent to its next major peak. Note that there was no real net upside

Chart 7-3   Commodity price lows versus the economy, 1970–1981. (*Source: pring.com*)

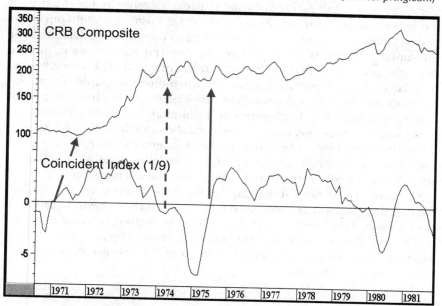

progress between 1974 and 1975. The reason for the low in 1974 lay in the fact that the previous bottom had encouraged huge amounts of speculation, and as prices fell, these same speculators were forced out at any price by a huge wave of margin calls. This meant that commodities were being liquidated well below their true economic value. The temporary oversupply was quickly corrected, and prices bounced back in mid-1974. However, until a reversal in the economy results in a more substantial demand for commodities, prices made little net upside progress.

This unusual 1974 experience can be compared to that of 1971, when commodity prices did not bottom until the recovery was well underway. This can be appreciated from the rightward-sloping arrow that connects the zero crossover point of the coincident indicator with that of the late 1971 low in commodity prices.

Bond Prices Peak   At this point, all three markets are in a rising trend. However, every good party comes to an end, and this one is no exception, as the period of falling interest rates draws rapidly to a close. Gradually, the reported economic data improve, and it becomes evident that the recovery has taken hold. The Central Bank abandons its role as recession fighter. Monetary policy at this stage does not immediately move to one of tightness but more toward neutrality. At the same time, businesses and consumers become more confident and become willing to take on more debt. Because the supply of credit is less expansive and demand has increased, interest rates (the price of credit) bottom out. Interest rate troughs are usually gradual affairs, looking something like saucers when shown in graphic form. This contrasts with cyclical peaks, which are associated with the frenzied pace of borrowing activity that characterizes the involuntary inventory accumulation phase and are, therefore, much sharper, parabolic affairs. Chart 7-4 features the deflationary 1990s, where the contrast between the slow-rounding bottoms and the spiky tops is self-evident. Interest rate peaks in the inflationary 1970s and 1980s were more dramatic than those shown here.

The gently rising rates at this stage in the cycle reflect stable, controlled, but definitely improving business conditions and do not adversely affect the stock market. This is because equity investors are focusing on corporate profits. Provided they are anticipated to expand at a faster clip than interest rates and rising rates are not perceived as a threat to the recovery, the stock market continues to advance.

Chart 7-4   The 3-month Commercial Paper Yield, tops versus bottoms, 1981–2000. (*Source: pring.com*)

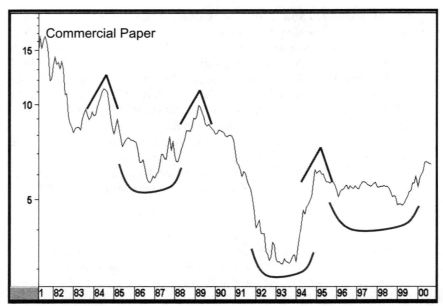

Equities Peak   At some point, though, rising rates do adversely affect the economy, and stock market participants anticipate potential economic weakness, selling equities in a similar way to which they had earlier purchased them as the recovery was being discounted. Even though stocks are falling, the economy itself continues to expand, using up what little excess manufacturing and labor market capacity that still exists. As a result, demand for commodities outstrips the available supply. Through the mechanism of the free market, quantities are then rationed by higher prices.

Chart 7-5 shows the relationship between the stock market and the economy, as measured by the 9-month moving-average deviation of the coincident indicators featured earlier. This time we are looking at the characteristics of the economy at market peaks. Notice how the stock market peaks between the late 1950s and 1980 were all closely associated with peak-readings in the economic oscillator, virtually without exception. Chart 7-6 shows that the 1981 and 1983 peaks operated in a similar manner. After that point, there were no recessions, except 1990. Consequently, the 1988 peak in the coincident indicators was not associated with a stock market top, which had developed earlier in 1987. The 1990 equity peak was on track, but the eco-

Chart 7-5   Stock market highs versus the economy, 1957–1980. (*Source: pring.com*)

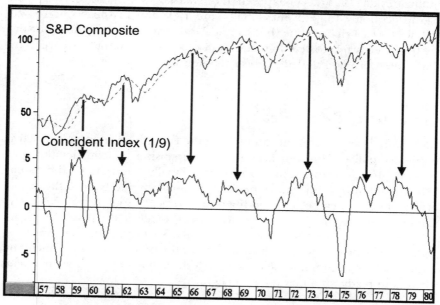

Chart 7-6 Stock market highs versus the economy, 1978–2000. (*Source: pring.com*)

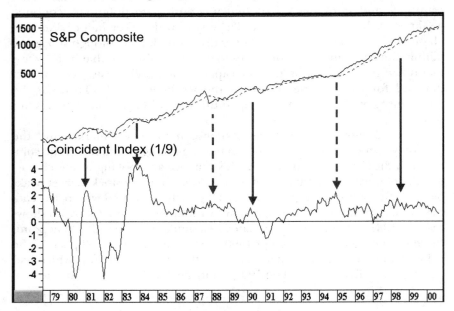

nomic peak of 1994 was juxtaposed to the market, which bottomed as soon as the economy topped out. Finally, the 1998 top in the economy was followed by a brief decline, but by and large, the market throughout the 1990s correctly forecasted no recession. Consequently, it was not surprising that there were no full-fledged bear markets á la the 1970s.

Commodity Prices Peak

Eventually, inflation gets the attention of the Fed, which adopts a restrictive monetary policy. This and a continued expansion in loan demand put renewed upward pressure on interest rates. Finally, the strain on the system brought about by higher rates succeeds in breaking the back of the recovery. In turn, this causes commodity prices to peak. Sometimes, this event takes place at the tail end of the recovery, occasionally in the first few months of the recession. Chart 7-7 shows that the CRB Spot Industrial Raw Material Index generally makes its peak either side of the point when the coincident indicator momentum falls below zero. All three markets are now in a bear phase and ready for a new cycle to begin.

Chart 7-7 CRB Spot Raw industrial prices versus the economy, 1972–1993. (*Source: pring.com*)

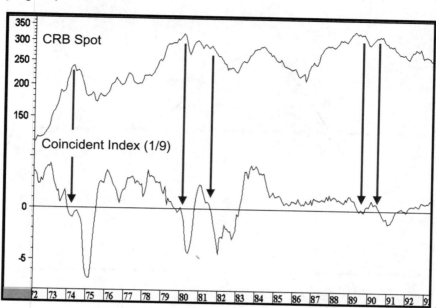

The Double Cycle

You may recall that I earlier used the terminology *growth recession* and *double cycle*. These situations develop when the trough between recessions extends well beyond the normal 41-month periodicity. In this event, the economy and financial markets undergo what I call a *double cycle,* where the contraction in business activity is replaced by *a slowdown in the growth rate,* rather than a contraction. A hypothetical example is shown in Fig. 7-3. You can see how the economic activity peaks and then declines but does not fall below the equilibrium level, that is, does not fall into a recession. Instead, the growth rate bottoms just above zero and then reverses to the upside again. In economic jargon, this phenomenon is known as a *growth recession.* It has developed more frequently in the postwar era, due to the commitment of governments to a full-employment policy. Interestingly, the financial market sequence described above also occurs during the double cycle. An example is shown in Fig. 7-4, where the same bond-stock-commodity sequence takes place. One difference between the normal and the double cycle is that bear markets in equities tend to be more constrained and bull markets larger. Also, the growth recession bottom is associated with a faster progression, as the leads are much shorter.

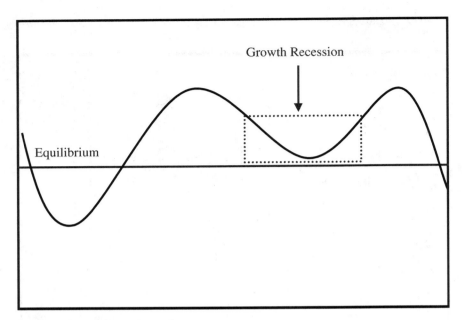

Figure 7-3 An idealized growth recession.

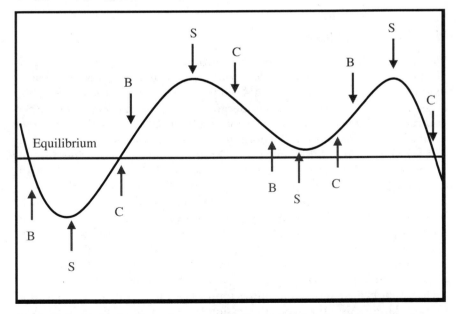

Figure 7-4 Idealized peaks and troughs of the financial markets in a growth recession.

An example of a double cycle occurred in the 1980s during the so-called *rolling recession.* All sectors and regions of the United States moved into the recovery stage in the early 1980s, but by the 1985–1986 period, the farm, energy-producing, and rust-belt areas of the country experienced an extremely sharp recession. Because other regions were quite buoyant, the aggregate economy did not slip into recession, but the internal distortions were so great that the financial markets experienced a couple of mini-cycles. This period is shown in Chart 7-8, where the S&P Composite is once again compared with the coincident indicators expressed as a deviation from a 9-month moving average. The two dashed vertical arrows show the approximate points of the 1982 and 1990 recessions. The coincident oscillator traces out a rough double cycle. This consists of a recovery (A), followed by a reaction into the mid-1980s (B) but no actual recession. Then another recovery move into the late 1980s (C), followed by another down-move into the 1990 recession (D).

Chart 7-9 shows the three markets—money market prices, stocks, and commodities—over the same period. Once again, the two small vertical arrows flag the approximate recession points. The other arrows join the cyclical turning points. The solid arrows between 1984 and 1986 join the double cycle lows. Note that this final set of peaks does not quite develop

Chart 7-8 S&P Composite versus the economy, 1982–1990. (*Source: pring.com*)

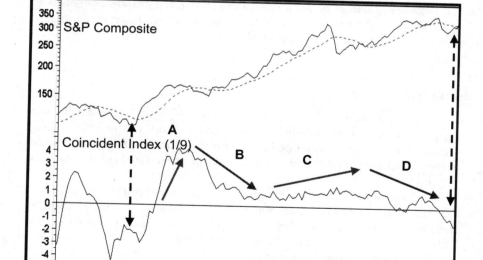

Chart 7-9 Three financial markets, 1980–1993. (*Source: pring.com*)

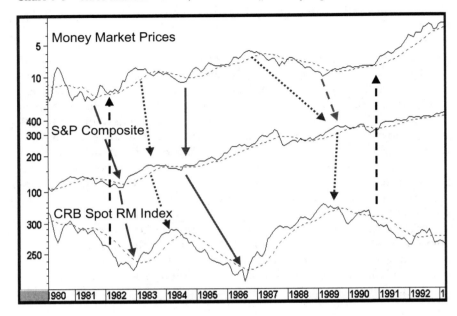

in the idealized way. This is because the money market series bottoms before the 1989 stock market peak, and stocks peak after commodities. This is an unusual set of circumstances and reflects the very deflationary environment that was prevalent during this period.

The Six Stages

We have established the fact that in most business cycles, there is a chronological sequence between bonds, stocks, and commodity prices. Since there are three markets and each one has two turning points, it follows that so far as these particular markets are concerned, there are six stages to the business cycle.

These are shown in Fig. 7-5. Stage I starts when bond prices bottom, Stage II is where stocks bottom, and Stage III develops when commodities start their bull market. Then the bears start to take over and bond prices peak. This gives us Stage IV. Eventually, stocks peak out for Stage V. Finally, commodities reverse to the downside as the cycle emerges into Stage VI, when all three markets are in retreat.

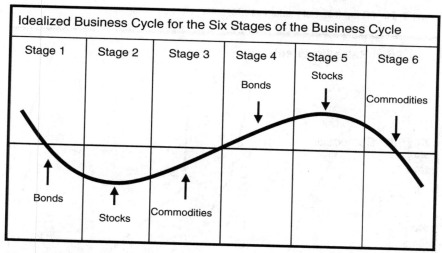

Figure 7-5 The six stages.

We now have a framework from which to operate. The trick, of course, is to figure out the prevailing stage of the cycle and then select the appropriate industry groups and stocks. I use models based on financial, economic, and technical indicators, called *barometers,* to help me obtain a better fix on this, and I feature them each month in my *Intermarket Newsletter.*[2] However, if you do not have access to this information, a possible substitute is to relate the three markets to their respective 12-month moving averages. When a specific market is above its average, it is classified as bullish, and vice versa. Chart 7-10 demonstrates how it might have worked in the early 1980s. In late 1981, the cycle was in a Stage I, as money market prices crossed their 12-month MA. This is then followed by stocks in late 1982 and finally by commodities, as they, too, joined the other markets in a positive trend. Then, in mid-1983, money market prices peak out, followed by stocks and commodities. A new Stage I began in October 1984, but stocks moved out of sequence and preceded money market prices. However, if we take a decisive 12-month MA crossover (as at point A) as our signal, the S&P does move within the expected sequence. Finally, it is not until late 1986 that commodities signaled a Stage III. Then we see a peak in money market prices for a new Stage IV. The 1987 cash gives us a Stage V, and as the chart ends, we await the Stage VI crossover by the commodity index. Actually, I have

[2]Details at *pring.com.*

Chart 7-10 Three financial markets, 1980–1987. (*Source: pring.com*)

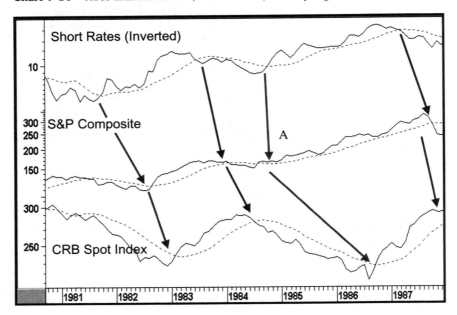

cheated a bit with this chart because the S&P quickly rallied back above its MA prior to the bottoming in money market prices. This out-of-sequence event was unusual, but it is important to understand that such exceptions definitely happen from time to time.

Apart from the 1987 experience, that was a fairly logical and straightforward period, more or less typical of the previous 200 years. However, as we move on to the 1990s in Chart 7-11, things became more complicated for two reasons. First, the economy did not experience a recession. Indeed, growth was slow and consistent and did not result in much of a double cycle. Remember, *it is the fluctuations in the economy that give us the inflationary and deflationary swings.* If the economy does not experience much of a boom/bust cycle, neither will the markets. If the business cycle is dead and the economy no longer experiences moderate swings, then this form of analysis will no longer work. However, the business cycle is a reflection of human nature, which operates between the two pendulum points of fear and greed. I doubt whether much has, or will, change in this direction in the next few decades. Second, the stock market experienced its strongest and longest bull market in recorded history, largely due to merger and

Chart 7-11 Three financial markets, 1989–2001. (*Source: pring.com*)

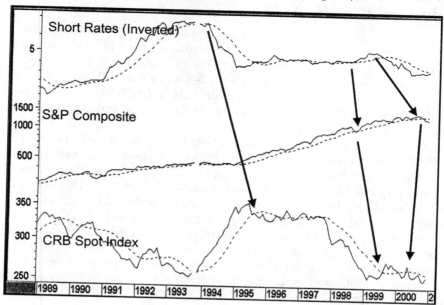

acquisition activity and an unprecedented technological boom. That meant that there were no real bear markets that would fit comfortably in the six stage analysis.

When you look at it in perspective, the money market series was in a bear market from late 1994 until 1998. The stock market, which had a life of its own, went completely out of sequence and crossed above its 12-month MA in 1995. In the meantime, it is possible to draw a dashed arrow connecting the negative MA crossover of the money market series to a similar crossover by the CRB Commodity Index. At the end of 1998, things seem to come back in gear, since the money market series crosses above its average for a Stage I, stocks quickly follow suit for Stage II and commodities do the same for a very short Stage III. Finally, early 1999 sees money market prices crack their moving average for a Stage IV, stocks in mid 2000 for a Stage V, and almost simultaneously, commodities make it a Stage VI. In terms of the bond-stock-commodity chronology, the late 1980s and most of the 1990s are by far the most confusing period I have ever seen from over 200 years of history. If the business cycle returns to its normal cyclical swings in the twenty-first century, I have no doubt that the chronology will, as well.

The Characteristics of Primary Bull and Bear Markets

There is one more aspect of trend and business cycles that I would like to cover before we look at the actual group rotation process, and that is the secular or very long term trend. Just as the direction of the primary trend influences the magnitude of short-term 2–6–week fluctuations, so the secular trend affects the character of the primary trend. Typically, the secular trend embraces three or four or more primary trends and lasts anywhere from 10 to 30 years.

Chart 7-12, featuring corporate bond yields, demonstrates the point well. The last 70 years of the twentieth century were dominated by three secular trends. The first was a downtrend during the 1930s and 1940s. Then an inflationary uptrend developed between the mid-1940s and 1981. This was then followed by another deflationary secular trend at the end of the century. Generally speaking, during the inflationary sequence of the long wave, bull markets in commodities and bond yields tend to be fairly lengthy, whereas bear markets are relatively short (Chart 7-13). The tables are completely turned when the deflationary wave takes over. In this instance, bear markets are very long and experience substantial magnitude, and the counter-

Chart 7-12   Bond Yields and the secular trend, I. (*Source: pring.com*)

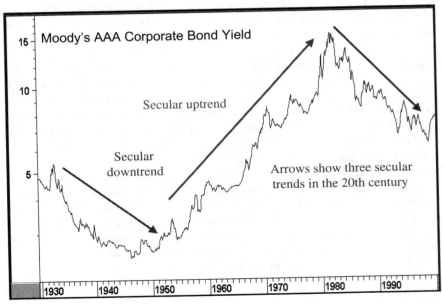
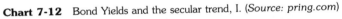

Chart 7-13   Bond Yields and the secular trend, II. (*Source: pring.com*)

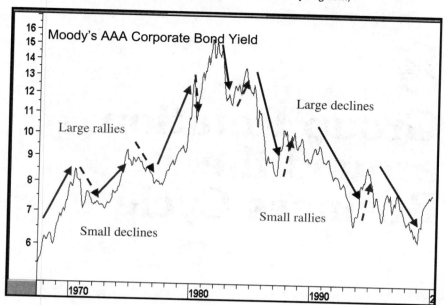

cyclical rallies are relatively brief. We shall discover later that each business cycle has an inflationary and deflationary part, just like the long wave. Consequently, during a secular or very long term inflationary environment, the inflationary portion of the business cycle predominates, but in the down-wave, it is the deflationary part that experiences greater magnitude and duration. This means that inflation-dominated cycles are usually associated with superior performance by energy and mining stocks, but in the down-wave, the stellar performers tend to be concentrated in the defensive areas. Natural beneficiaries include issues such as foods, financials, interest-sensitive and other defensive groups. This environment is also favorable, of course, for bonds.

8
Group Rotation around the Business Cycle

The Cycle Divided into Inflationary and Deflationary Parts

Now that we have an understanding of the chronological sequence of economic events that develops during a typical business cycle, we are in a better position to appreciate how the performance of industry groups is affected by the prevailing business cycle environment. The six-stage approach to the business cycle has already been discussed, but it is also possible to simplify this even more by dividing the cycle into an inflationary one after the recovery gets underway and a deflationary one during the contractionary phase and at the start of the recovery, as in Fig. 8-1. The magnitude and duration of the inflation or deflation in any cycle will depend largely on the direction of the secular trend. For example, in the inflationary postwar period between the late 1940s and 1981, the inflation part of the cycle predominated. Between 1981 and the turn of the century, it was deflation's turn. Inflation, as measured by the CPI, was predominant throughout this whole period, of course. When I speak of inflation or deflation, I am referring to inflationary and deflationary forces as reflected in the primary trends of bond yields and industrial commodity prices.

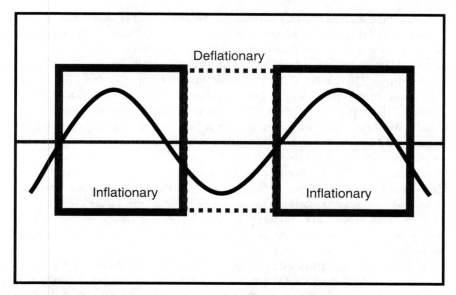

Figure 8-1 The inflationary and deflationary part of the business cycle.

Extending our idea of these two parts of the business cycle, it is even possible to construct some indexes that reflect inflation- and deflation-sensitive groups and express them as a ratio. Determining the current phase of the cycle then becomes a relatively simple matter. I will have more to say on that later.

First, though, let us consider what happens after the economy has been in a contractionary phase for a couple of months. It has already been established that bond prices bottom out and interest rates begin to fall (Fig. 7-2). But it is also important to understand that there are certain stock groups that do well when interest rates are declining. These are known as *early cycle leaders* or *liquidity-driven groups,* because they benefit from the new trend of lower interest rates. Utilities and banks and other financials come to mind—utilities, because they are capital intensive and have to borrow huge amounts of money. Falling interest rates lower their costs and boost profits. Utilities also pay relatively large dividends. When interest rates fall, these high-yielding stocks become more competitive with stocks paying low dividends, and so their prices rise or, at the tail end of a bear market, fall less rapidly. There is also a psychological element because utility earnings are relatively easy to predict, and the generous dividends make them a safe haven when other equity prices are taking a battering.

Financials, such as banks, insurance companies, and brokers, also start to bottom at the time of the interest rate peak—banks, because the cost of their principal product comes down when interest rates decline. Also, banks are slower to lower their lending costs than their borrowing costs that finance the lendings. This means that their profit margins improve. Insurance companies have huge portfolios of bonds. When rates decline, this inflates the values of these portfolios and makes insurance companies more attractive. Finally, brokers make more money in a bull market, since commissions expand and underwriting fees from IPOs increase, as more companies come to market when equity prices are high.

A final group that bottoms out at this stage of the cycle is consumer nondurables. This sector includes things such as tobacco, beverages, personal care, and food manufactures. The earnings of these companies are relatively easy to predict, they are relatively safe, and relatively more immune from recession than the more economically sensitive big ticket items, such as autos and other consumer durables.

Basic industry, technology, and resource-based issues do best at the other end of the cycle. These are known as *late cycle leaders* or *earnings-driven groups* and tend to outperform the market once commodity prices have bottomed (Fig. 8-2). Please remember, though, that this is not an exact science and that the actual bottoms for these groups can vary considerably. The good news is that their *relative* performance *tends* to be much easier to predict. As the cycle matures and capacity tightens, these corporations find that their customers are willing to pay more for their products, and so they can easily raise prices. These price increases immediately go to the bottom line, boosting profits and making them more attractive. Also, as capacity tightens, corporations embark on ambitious capital equipment expansion projects. This also increases the demands for the products produced by basic industry and technology companies.

Inflation- versus Deflation-Sensitive Groups

I mentioned in the previous clip that it is possible to construct a leading group and a lagging group. They are shown in Chart 8-1. The Deflation Group Index is featured in the top panel, and the Inflation Group Index is in the lower one. The deflation series is constructed from liquidity-driven issues, such as utilities, property casualty insurers, and savings and loans.

The Inflation Group is constructed from the S&P Aluminums, Domestic Oils, Miscellaneous Mines, and Gold. There is nothing remarkable about this chart, but when I construct a ratio by dividing the inflation by the

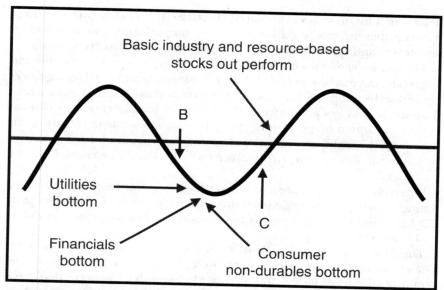

Figure 8-2 Group performance at various stages in the cycle.

Chart 8-1 The inflation versus the deflation group index. (*Source: pring.com*)

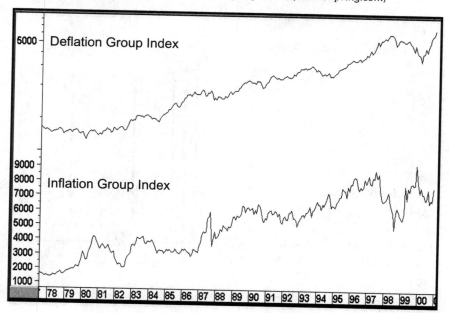

deflation, a useful series is displayed (Chart 8-2). When the ratio is rising, it means that inflation-sensitive groups are outperforming their deflation-sensitive counterparts. When it is declining, the deflations are winning.

The direction of the ratio has important implications for both asset allocation and individual stock purchase and sale. When it is rising, it means that lagging stocks are outperforming leading stocks. However, because this is a *relative* relationship, it does not guarantee that either party is advancing or declining, merely that one is outperforming the other. (It is possible to construct this ratio from the real-time version of MetaStock using formulas and data contained in the *Martin Pring How to Select Stocks MetaStock Companion CD-ROM Tutorial.*)

Reversals in the ratio are not only important from the point of view of timing a change in the cycle from the deflationary to the inflationary part, but have important implications for the course of bond yields and industrial commodity prices.

This is where the 12-month ROC in the lower panel can be of help. The arrows mark the points where the ROC, having rallied to the +−40 percent dashed horizontal line, then crosses below it. It is apparent that these signals roughly correspond to the peak in the inflation/deflation ratio. This approach works well because the inflation- and deflation-sensitive groups are

Chart 8-2   The inflation/deflation ratio, 1957–2001. (*Source: pring.com*)

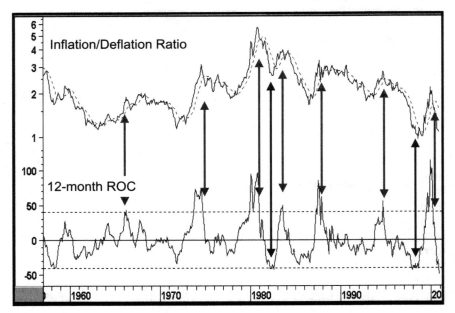

continually trading places with each other, as the business cycle progresses. Rarely does this relationship form a linear or secular trend; it is very cyclical.

It is useful because it tells us what view stock market participants have about the future course of these two stock groups and because reversals in the ratio are related to primary trend changes in bond yields and industrial commodity prices.

How the Stock Market Forecasts Trends in Yields and Commodity Prices

Chart 8-3 compares the performance of the inflation/deflation ratio against government bond yields and industrial commodity prices. The broad swings in the ratio are not dissimilar to those of the bond yield in the center panel and the CRB Spot Raw Industrial Material Index in the lower panel. I have highlighted the inflationary secular trend with solid lines and the deflationary one with dashed ones. The exact copy for the inflation/deflation

Chart 8-3 The inflation/deflation ratio versus bond yields and commodity prices, 1957–2001. (*Source: pring.com*)

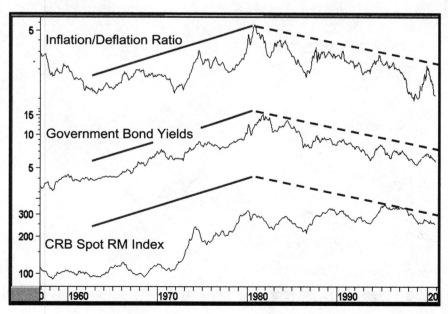

ratio has been placed over the bond yield and commodity series. You can see that there is a reasonably close fit, especially for the yield series. Chart 8-4 repeats the same exercise but this time for business cycle associated swings. They, too, line up reasonably closely. Obviously, they are not exact replicas, especially since an allowance needs to be made for the fact that commodity prices lead bond yields. But the connection between the three series is undeniable.

Chart 8-5 compares these same three series again, but this time the arrows that were associated with the 12-month ROC overbought crossovers for the inflation/deflation ratio in Chart 8-2 have been overlaid. The purpose of this exercise is to demonstrate that momentum reversals in the ratio can be used to identify primary-trend reversals in bond yields and commodity prices. The first crossover developed in the mid-1960s. It was premature for the ratio itself and was totally useless for a bond-yield sell signal. However, it was spot on for commodity prices. As time progresses, this technique improves in accuracy, since nearly all of the arrows flag at least one peak. What is happening is that market participants, by buying and selling infla-

Chart 8-4 The inflation/deflation ratio versus bond yields and commodity prices, 1957–2001. (*Source: pring.com*)

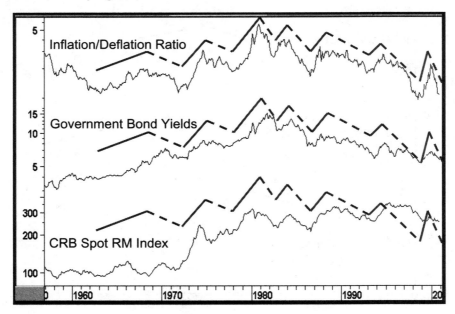

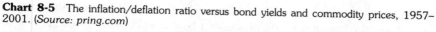

Chart 8-5 The inflation/deflation ratio versus bond yields and commodity prices, 1957–2001. (*Source: pring.com*)

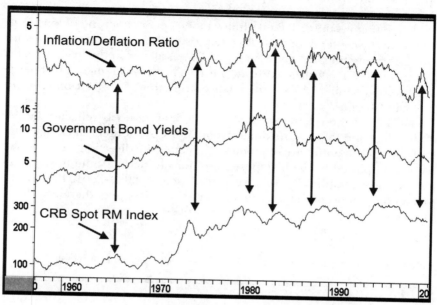

tion- and deflation-sensitive equities, are correctly identifying peaks in interest rates and commodity prices. Since yields and commodity prices are an integral part of the economy, there is a direct connection with the price performance of leading and lagging groups.

Leading/Lagging Group Relationships

I realize that many readers will not be able to construct the inflation/deflation ratio. However, I think it was an instructive exercise, even if it is just to prove that there is a definite inflation/deflation battle continually evolving in the stock market cycle. The next series of charts will just use two industry groups, one as a proxy for leading, and the other for lagging, sectors. This type of analysis is simple enough to apply in most of the popular charting software packages, such as the End of Day, MetaStock, TC 2000, and so on. These relationships are not quite as accurate as the inflation/deflation ratio but are certainly useful from the point of view of analyzing major trend changes in the group rotation process and can also be used for timing major market turning points.

Chart 8-6 shows the S&P Banks Index in the upper panel and its long-term RS line in the center. When the RS line is rising, it means that the banks are outperforming the S&P, and vice versa. The oscillator in the lower panel is a long-term KST constructed from the RS line. This momentum series is overlaid on a similar KST for the relative strength of the S&P Domestic Oil Index in Chart 8-7.

The KST of the relative strength of the bank index is reflected by the dashed line and that for the domestic oil index by the solid thick one. It is fairly obvious that they are often moving in opposite directions. The arrows have been placed in the juxtaposed positions to demonstrate this characteristic more graphically. In rare cases, such as 2000–2001, they move together, but most of the time their courses are diverging, thereby indicating the existence of the group rotation process.

Chart 8-6   S&P banks and relative strength, 1976–2001. (*Source: pring.com*))

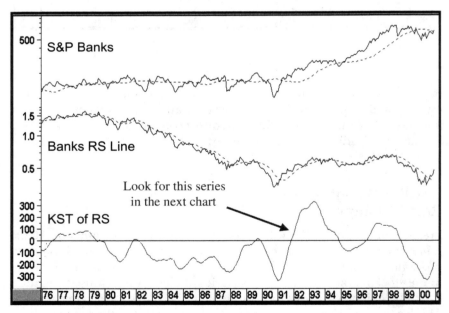

Chart 8-7 Banks versus Oils Relative Momentum, 1944–2001.

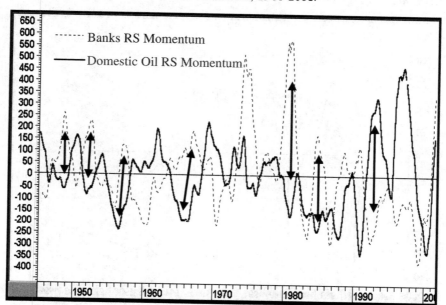

Chart 8-8 shows a similar arrangement, but this time it is the S&P Financials and the S&P Energy Indexes that are being compared. Once again, the two are diverging in their paths most of the time. One interesting point is that the three occasions when the energy has crossed above the financials, the stock market has subsequently experienced a serious setback. The first was in the summer of 1987, the second just prior to the 1990 mini-bear market. The third at the end of 1999 preceded the peak in the NAS-DAQ by a few months, after which it lost over 60 percent of its value. In all these situations, the crossing therefore warned that equity prices were in the terminal phase of a bull market.

Another useful relationship is that between financials and technology. Chart 8-9 features the relative KSTs for both. The arrows show when the financials bottom and technology peaks, whereas the arrows in Chart 8-10 indicate when the computers bottom and the financials peak.

Chart 8-8 Financial versus energy relative momentum, 1985–2000. (*Source: pring.com*)

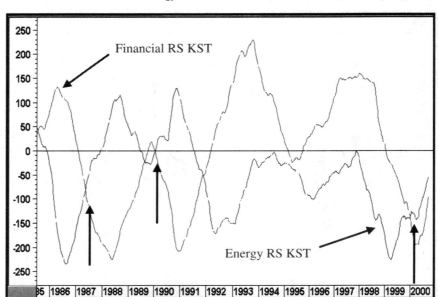

Chart 8-9 Computer versus financial relative momentum, 1976–2001. (*Source: pring.com*)

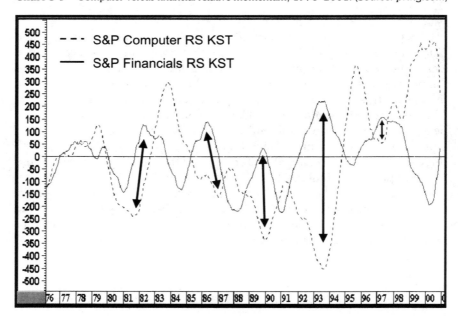

Chart 8-10   Computer versus financial relative momentum, 1976–2001. (*Source: pring.com*)

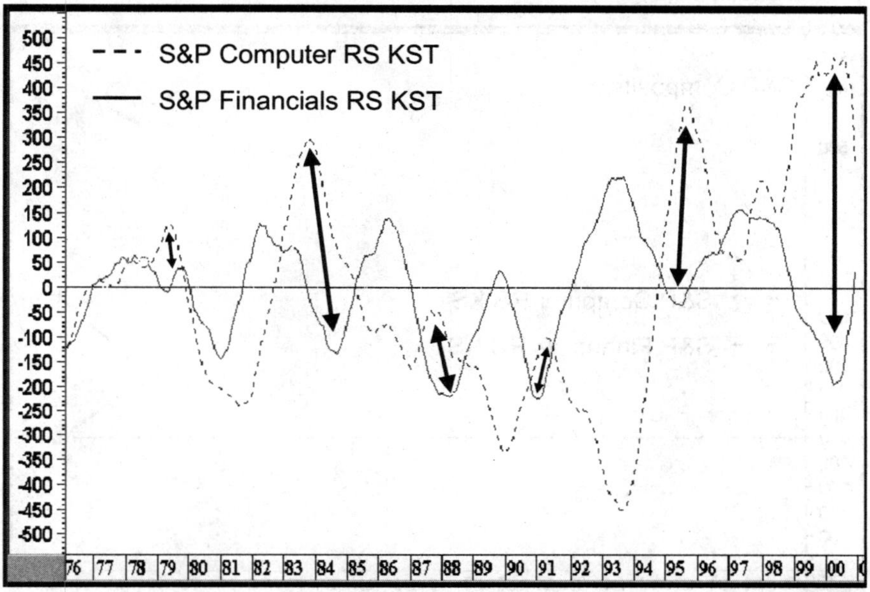

Finally, Chart 8-11 shows the same two relative KSTs featured along with the S&P Composite. Note how the huge bull market between 1997 and 1999 was powered by very strong relative momentum in the tech sector, whereas the financials declined. (Incidentally, they also declined on an absolute basis.) The exact opposite happened when the NASDAQ bubble burst because it was the financials that dominated in the latter part of the year 2000 and for the first half of 2001.

It is also interesting to note that the bottoms in the S&P Financial relative KST have usually been followed by a positive environment for stocks in general. This is demonstrated in Chart 8-12 by the vertical arrows. There was one major exception that developed in 1981, yet even in this instance, a substantial number of stocks rallied. The averages, though, were weighed down by a weak performance in the lagging groups. That more than offset strength in the leading sectors.

Chart 8-11 Computer and financial relative momentum versus the S&P Composite, 1979–2000. (*Source: pring.com*)

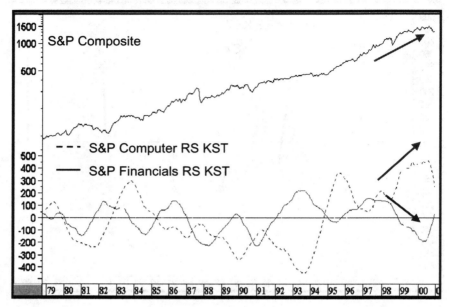

Chart 8-12 Computer and financial relative momentum versus the S&P Composite, 1979–2000. (*Source: pring.com*)

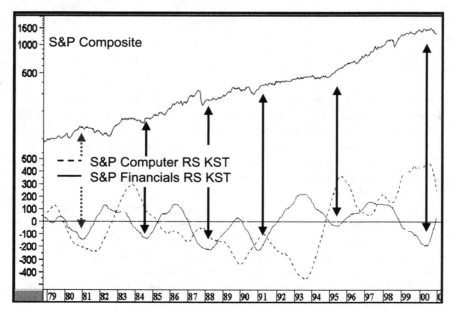

Before we leave this idea of using relative momentum to identify stock market bottoms, there is one more relationship to cover, and that is between banks, an early leader, and aluminums, a laggard. This ratio is represented in Chart 8-13. In this instance, a *rising* line is *deflationary* because it means that banks are outperforming the aluminums, and vice versa. The arrows flag the major stock market bottoms since the 1950s. Pretty well all of them develop close to a low in the bank/aluminum ratio, except the 1982 experience. Unfortunately, we know only with the benefit of hindsight which bottom in the indicator corresponds with a major stock market low. However, there is a way around this dilemma and that is to calculate a long-term KST of the ratio and wait for the KST to cross above its 9-month MA. This is shown in Chart 8-14 for the 1960s and 1970s. The arrows have been drawn exactly at the stock market lows. It is evident that this is not an exact science, but it is reasonable to expect a market bottom either a bit before the KST bottoms or a little after. Unfortunately, there are two exceptions that are flagged by the two dashed arrows. Interestingly, neither was associated with recessions.

Chart 8-15 brings us up to the close of the last century. Once again, the KST reversals offer pretty good signals.

Chart 8-13 Computer and financial relative momentum versus the S&P Composite, 1979–2000. (*Source: pring.com*)

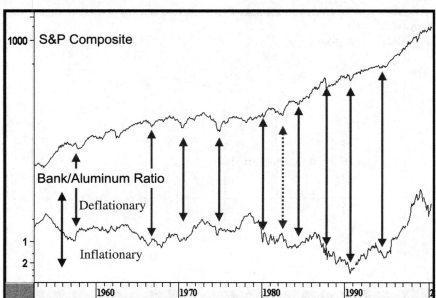

Chart 8-14 Bank/aluminum ratio versus the S&P Composite, 1952–2000. (*Source: pring.com*)

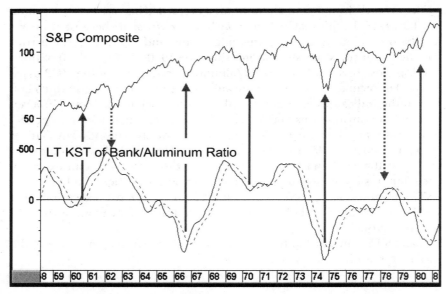

Chart 8-15 Bank/aluminum ratio momentum versus the S&P Composite, 1968–1981. (*Source: pring.com*)

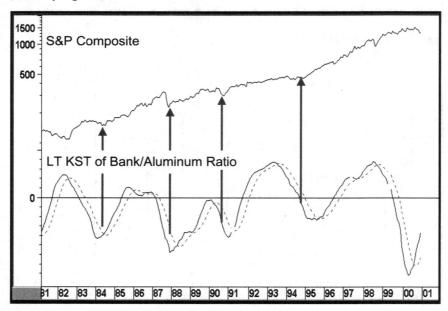

So far, we have concentrated more on using these relationships to identify the prevailing stage of the cycle. Now we must move on and demonstrate
how they can be adapted for the purposes of identifying positive groups and
bullish stocks within those groups.

9

Selecting Groups and Stocks at Major Turning Points

The Top-Down Approach

One of the most widely used methods of selecting stocks is the so-called *top-down approach*. This consists of identifying a good buying opportunity in the market as a whole, then isolating some industry groups buying candidates, and finally searching for stocks within those selected groups. This is a fairly systematic technique, where selections are not made in a random fashion but in a way in which stocks within groups act as a cross-check on each other. For example, you may do a scan on 2000 stocks and come up with, say, General Motors. It is possible that there is some special circumstance that is driving the price of GM. However, if you can identify the auto group as a buy candidate, and then observe that all, or pretty well all, of the stocks in the group are in a buying mode, then there is a clear-cut pattern to the whole picture. In this case, the buy signals are likely to be far more reliable because of the general move to auto stocks, as opposed to a specific technical condition isolated in one stock.

In the following example, we will assume that our market buying opportunity is a bear market bottom, as opposed to an intermediate low. As a result, it should be expected that market leadership is focused on the liquidity-driven groups, such as the financials, utilities, and consumer staples. Please note that all the signals we are looking at should be for trends lasting at least 6 to 9 months. Anything less than that in this exercise is really a failure. Since the charts we shall be viewing all cover a number of years, some of these rallies may look to be quite brief. However, if you look at the dates carefully, you will see that most of them usually last for at least a year.

We begin by isolating a market bottom. In this case, it is the late 1994 low. Obviously, this is being done with the benefit of hindsight, but we are assuming that there were enough technical signs to identify the bottom. With that in mind, we need to look at some early leader stock groups to see what they were doing.

Multi-Line Insurers

Chart 9-1 shows the multi-line insurance group. Incidentally, this chart arrangement will be featured quite widely in future examples, so I will take a little time now to explain the concept.

Basically, the chart features two series and their respective KSTs from a primary trend perspective. The absolute price, together with its 65-week EMA, is featured in the upper two panels. This 65-week timeframe is far from perfect, but it appears to work reasonably well in most situations. Also, it does give some long-term perspective as to whether the price is in a bull or bear trend. The KST is calculated using the same timeframes as those discussed in Chapter 5. The difference is that this calculation is made from weekly data, so, for example, the 24-month time span is replaced by 104 weeks, that is, 2 years. Also, the moving averages for the calculation are based on the exponential rather than a simple smoothing. Because RS is of crucial importance for stock selection, the RS line is featured in the third panel with its 65-week EMA. The bottom panel shows the long-term KST of relative strength. Thus we have a quick overview of the long-term technical position of both the absolute and relative trends. I should add that if your charting software does not allow calculation and plotting of the KST, substitute a long-term trend deviation, stochastic, or smoothed version of the MACD instead. For example, try using a 15/36 trend-deviation indicator, as discussed in Chapter 4. Alternatively, it is possible to use a 6-month MA of an 18-month ROC.

Chart 9-1 Multi-line insurance and three indicators, 1985–2000. (*Source: pring.com*)

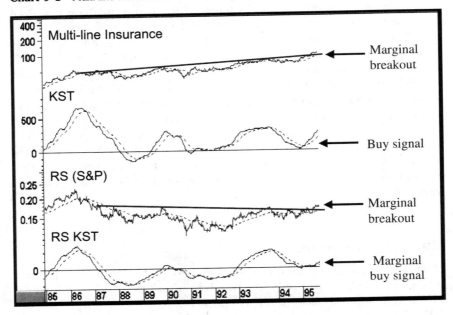

Referring back to Chart 9-1, you can see that the data from 1995 have been blotted out, so it is possible to appreciate what the picture looked like at that time. On an absolute basis, things looked pretty good. The price was in a bull trend because it was above its 65-week EMA and had experienced a series of rising peaks and troughs. Also, the long-term KST had just given a buy signal. Since the KST was decisively above its EMA at this time, we were left in no doubt as to the strong trend in long-term momentum. It was also possible to construct a major resistance trendline against the price itself. If an entry needed to be determined, a break above the line would have represented an excellent choice.

The relative line also broke above a resistance trendline and the relative KST had triggered a marginal buy signal. The bottom line here is that the multi-line insurers were okay to buy on both an absolute and relative basis. Chart 9-2 shows that this proved to be an accurate conclusion.

Property Casualty Insurers

The Property Casualty Insurance Index is another leading group. As you can see, the price in Chart 9-3 had already broken above a nice resistance trend-

Chart 9-2 Multi-line insurance and three indicators, 1985–2000. (*Source: pring.com*)

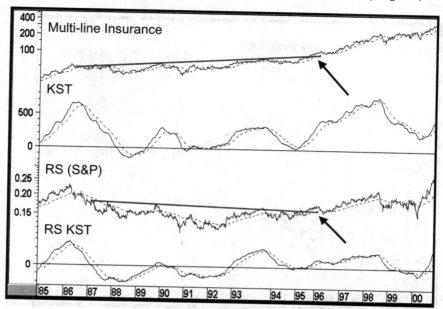

line, and the KST for the absolute price had not only gone bullish but had violated a downtrend line. The only problem was that these signals came from a moderately overbought condition. This meant that the price would not have to rise very much before an overbought reading would be registered. Generally speaking, we want to acquire stocks where the KSTs are both rising from below the zero level, thereby leaving lots of upside potential before they register an overbought condition.

At this time, the RS line was in a clear-cut uptrend, and the KST for relative strength had triggered a buy signal. Since our previous analysis indicated that the market had only just bottomed, this superior relative technical position told us that the property casualty insurers would continue to outperform the S&P Composite. Thus, while the moderately overbought reading in the absolute KST was a problem, the new buy signal by the relative KST told us not to worry, at least for the next few months.

Chart 9-4 unveils a bit more action, and you can see that the price continued to rally for about a year after. However, in the middle of 1996, the index violated its 65-week EMA and the KST generated a sell signal. Both the RS line and its KST also crossed below their respective EMAs. At this point, all series were negative and the KST of the absolute price was

Chart 9-3 Property casualty insurance and three indicators, 1988–2000. (*Source: pring.com*)

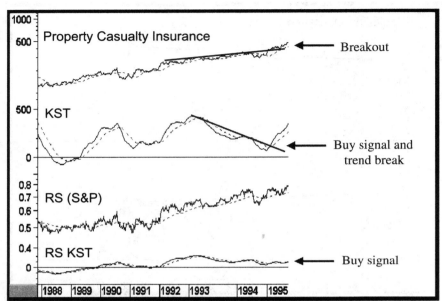

way overextended on the upside. Thus a sale would have been justified. Chart 9-4 then shows that the index did not decline: instead it moved in a long-term sideways trading range. Not too much damage here, but look at the RS line. It fell like a stone, indicating that there were far better opportunities elsewhere.

Now let us take a look at some of the property casualty stocks to see what they looked like at the time. Logic tells us to expect the majority of them looking in good shape. However, because groups have leaders and laggards within themselves, we often find that several stocks lead the actual index. This means that by the time the index gives a buy or sell signal, some stocks may already be overbought. Chart 9-5 of Acmat shows that the long-term KST for the absolute price was moderately overbought at the beginning of 1995. The price itself was in a trading range, so if it was able to rally above the resistance trendline, a buy signal would be triggered. However, it is important to note that the RS line and its KST were still bearish. This stock would be placed on our watch list as a potential buy candidate. Chart 9-6 displays more data and you can see that all four series eventually moved into bullish territory, thereby triggering a buy signal. The only problem lay in the fact that the absolute KST was moderately overbought when the signal developed. This did not preclude the price from moving higher, but it is

Chart 9-4 Property casualty insurance and three indicators, 1988–2000. (*Source: pring.com*)

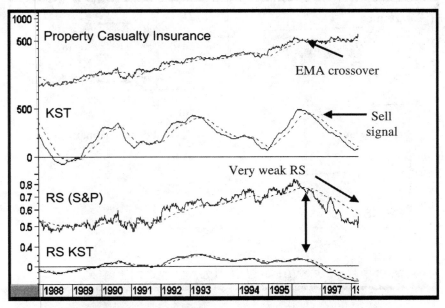

Chart 9-5 Acmat and three indicators, 1990–1997. (*Source: pring.com*)

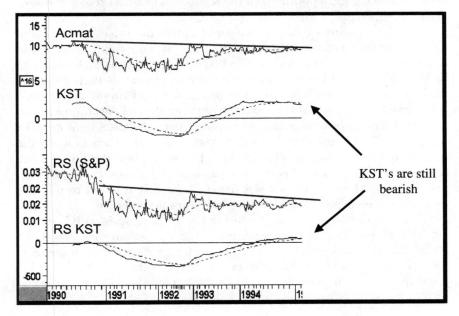

Chart 9-6   Acmat and three indicators, 1990–1997. (*Source: pring.com*)

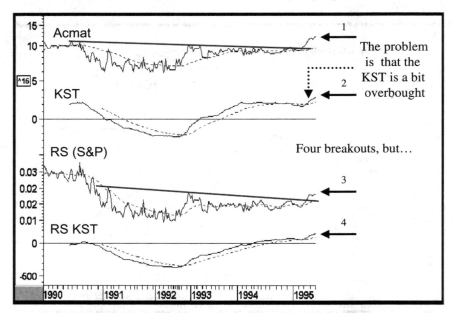

certainly not as good a position as if the KST was at or below zero and reversing to the upside.

As time passes, you can see what I mean in that the price, by the end of 1995 (Chart 9-7), is not much higher than the breakout point. Also, the RS line crosses below its EMA and the RS KST triggers a sell signal by violating its average. As it turned out, the price did move modestly higher but the trend of relative strength proved to be disappointing. I am not going to say that every KST buy signal that comes from a moderately overbought condition is followed by weak action such as this, because that is definitely not the case. In fact, some signals result in very strong price moves when the stock in question is in a secular uptrend. However, when the KST is moderately overbought, it means that the price does not have to move much higher before the odds favor a sell signal. If the KST is below zero, other things being equal, the price has a lot more upside potential.

The next example, Chart 9-8 featuring Ohio Casualty, shows it is important to keep monitoring a situation, even after a good buy signal has been given. This is because markets can, and do, change their minds. If the technical position is not the same as when you first bought a stock, what is the justification for continuing to hold it? Ohio Casualty looked to be in a prime

Chart 9-7 Acmat and three indicators, 1990–1997. (*Source: pring.com*)

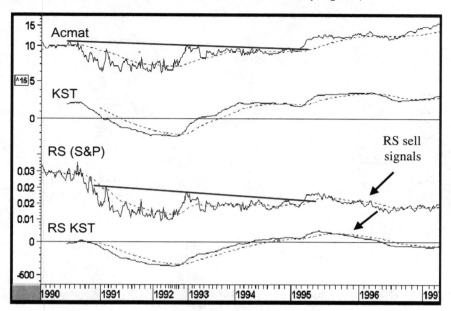

position at the start of 1995, since both KSTs had begun to rise from a position around zero. The price experienced a decisive breakout above its downtrend line, and the RS line a marginal breakout. However, in Chart 9-9 it is apparent that the RS breakout did not hold. Indeed, the KST for relative strength never did go bullish in the first place. The price itself falls back to support in the form of the extended downtrend line. Even though the absolute price trend remains positive, the weak RS performance indicates that there are better places to invest our money. Later on, we do see a price breakout. Both KSTs also go positive. However, the missing link is the RS line, which never rallies above this re-drawn downtrend line.

Old Republic (Chart 9-10), another casualty insurer, experienced a price and RS breakout at the start of 1995. At that point, both KSTs were still bearish. However, they had started to stabilize and were around the zero level. The trendline breaks, therefore, indicated that downside momentum was unlikely to extend, and that two KST buy signals should be expected. They did, in fact, materialize. Even when the RS line fell back to support in the form of the extended downtrend line, the KST for relative strength remained positive (Chart 9-11). As 1996 unfolds, Old Republic continued to extend its gains, but the RS line was basically flat, indicating a

Chart 9-8 Ohio Casualty and three indicators, 1991–1997. (*Source: pring.com*)

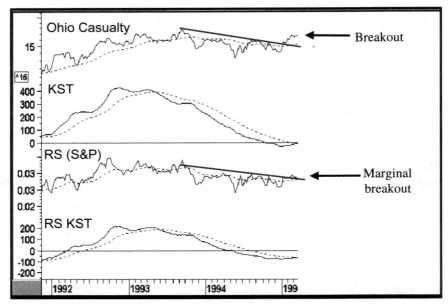

Chart 9-9 Ohio Casualty and three indicators, 1991–1997. (*Source: pring.com*)

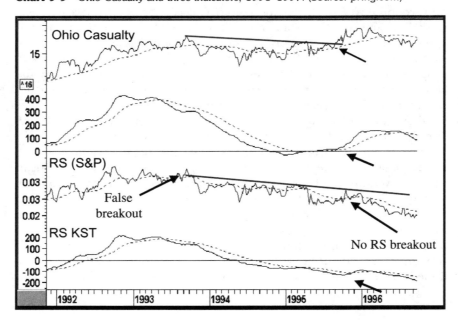

Chart 9-10 Old Republic and three indicators, 1992–1997. (*Source: pring.com*)

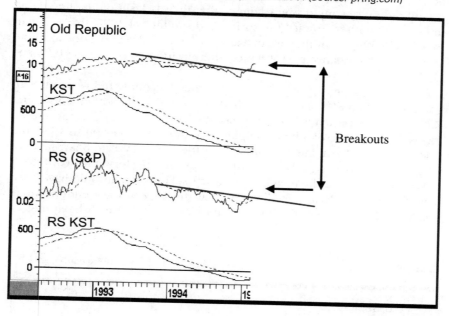

Chart 9-11 Old Republic and three indicators, 1992–1997. (*Source: pring.com*)

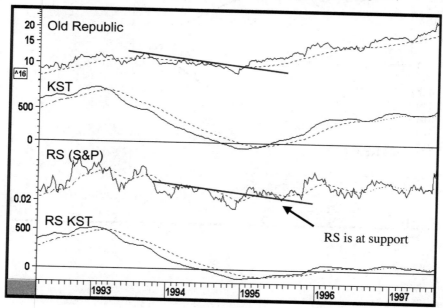

performance in line with the market. However, at no point during this period did we see any strong evidence that the stock should be liquidated in favor of another. Toward the spring and summer of 1996, things began to look a bit iffy, but by then we had already seen a full year of good absolute and reasonable relative performance, thereby justifying the early 1995 buy signals.

Finally, XL Capital (Chart 9-12) experienced a couple of breakouts with good supporting KST activity in early 1995. By mid-1996, both the price and RS lines had experienced very strong rallies (Chart 9-13). This more than meets our objective of a 9-month-plus time horizon. Later on in 1996, the price and RS lines violate trendlines, but the KSTs never go bearish. Thus we get some mixed signals. As it turned out, that performance continued to be quite strong in the next couple of years. However, it would have been perfectly reasonable to have liquidated at the time of the trendline violation, especially as the initial investment objective had already been met.

Chart 9-12   XL Capital and three indicators, 1993–1998. (*Source: pring.com*)

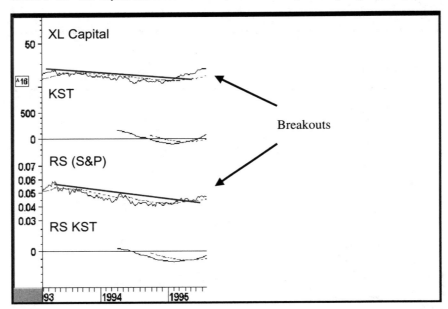

Chart 9-13 XL Capital and three indicators, 1993–1998. (*Source: pring.com*)

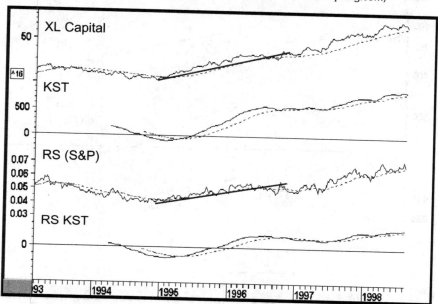

Brokerage Stocks

Security brokers have a tendency to make more profits during a bull market. This is because bull markets typically start when interest rates are declining. Since brokers finance a portfolio of securities, this means that their costs decline and the savings go straight to the bottom line. Volume and IPOs are also much greater during bull than bear markets, which means that commissions and underwriting fees are high. As a result, brokerage stocks have a tendency to lead the market both at tops and bottoms.

Chart 9-14 shows that at the start of 1995 both the absolute and relative price trends for the S&P Brokers break to the upside. The KSTs were still negative, but the positive trendline breaks indicated that downside momentum had dissipated and that a KST turn was likely. This was most definitely the case, but what of the stocks themselves? Merrill Lynch is the largest company in the group. It experienced two breakouts at the start of 1995 (Chart 9-15). This was later followed by a couple of KST buy signals. Not

Chart 9-14 Stock Brokers and three indicators, 1992–1996. (*Source: pring.com*)

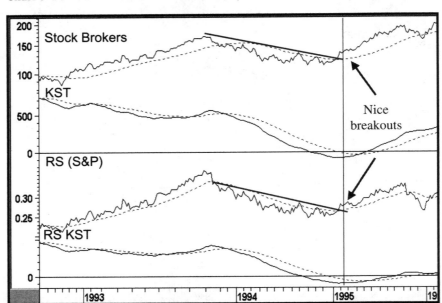

Chart 9-15 Merrill Lynch and three indicators, 1992–1998. (*Source: pring.com*)

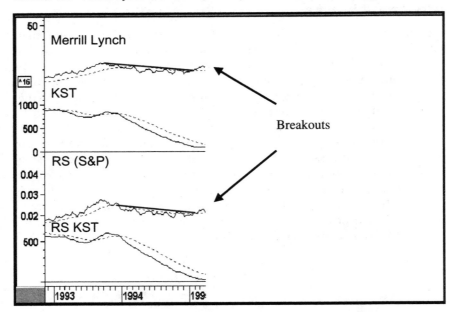

surprisingly, the stock outperformed the market for the next few months (Chart 9-16). Unfortunately, the RS line gave some false signs of a major weakness in fall 1995, which suggested switching to another group. This would have been a shame because the price went on to make a significant new high. However, it would have been possible to reenter the stock as the absolute and relative prices broke out in late 1996. The relative KST also went bullish. Since the absolute KST was quite overbought at the time, that would have tempered one's enthusiasm for the trade, which was a shame because it actually did quite well.

Both the absolute and relative lines for Advest broke out at the start of 1995 (Chart 9-17). Neither of the KSTs was bullish at this point, but they were so close that the trend breaks indicated a high probability that they would soon do so. Chart 9-18 indicates that this was soon to be the case. Advest proved to be an excellent investment, as the price continued to rally into 1996 and a little beyond. It was not until the end of 1996 that some signs of weakness began to develop. This proved to be a temporary interruption in an otherwise exceptionally strong trend.

Chart 9-16 Merrill Lynch and three indicators, 1992–1998. (*Source: pring.com*)

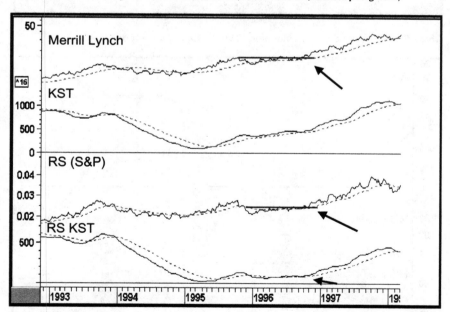

Chart 9-17   Advest and three indicators, 1992–1998. (*Source: pring.com*)

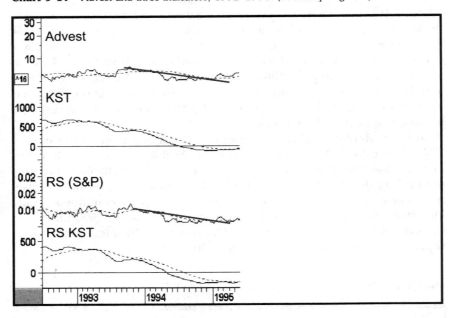

Chart 9-18   Advest and three indicators, 1992–1998. (*Source: pring.com*)

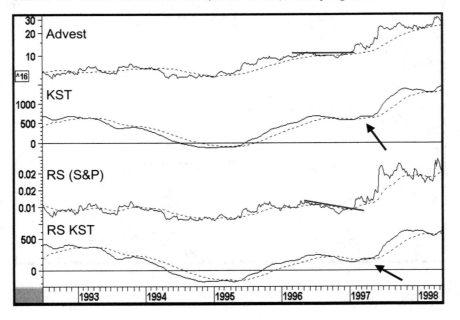

Chart 9-19 Raymond James and three indicators, 1992–1999. (*Source: pring.com*)

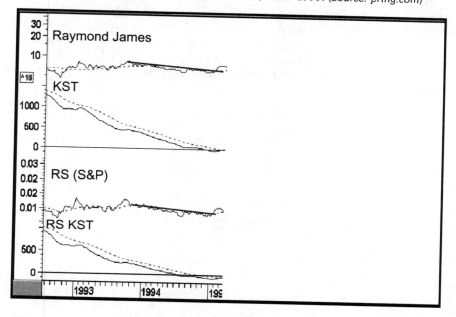

Chart 9-20 Raymond James and three indicators, 1992–1999. (*Source: pring.com*)

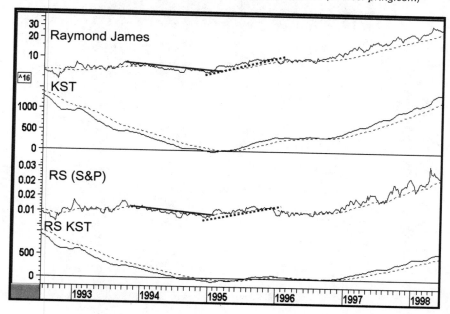

Finally, Raymond James (Chart 9-19) experienced a familiar pattern of a price and RS breakout, later to be followed by two positive KST signals. The positive trend lasted for several months, and then a joint violation of the absolute and RS dashed lines developed (Chart 9-20). This stock, just like Merrill and Advest, went on to make significant new highs, but at the time, these two trendbreaks would have mandated liquidation.

10
Using Changes in Strategic Relationships to Identify Rotational Leadership Changes

Property Casualty/ Aluminum RS Ratio

In the previous example, we identified a bull market bottom and used our group rotation analysis to identify groups and stocks that were appearing to emerge as leaders on a long-term basis. Now it is time to use a different technique. We have already learned that beneath the market averages there is a continual struggle for leadership between leading and lagging groups. Changes in leadership often develop at major market turning points, such as a bull market high or bear market low. However, they also develop in midstream, so to speak. In the stock selection process, we are concerned with identifying market leaders at an early stage and riding on that trend, provided we can also get some confirmation from the absolute price.

115

This next technique tries to identify when these long-term changes in leadership develop and then use the top-down approach to zero in on the groups and stocks that are likely to benefit.

This can be accomplished by comparing an early cycle (liquidity-driven) group, the property casualty insurers, and relating its performance to an earnings-driven group, the aluminums. The technique also involves using a ratio of their respective relative strength lines, which tend to be a little more cyclical than the ratio of the actual prices. Chart 10-1 shows that it is quite volatile, so I have plotted a long-term KST underneath.

Using the KST moving-average crossovers gives us some good signals of leadership changes. The sell signals are represented by the dashed arrows and the buys with the solid ones. Since this is a *relative* relationship, the sell in this case means a sell for the insurers relative to the aluminums. For the aluminums, it means a buy relative to the insurance stocks. In our earlier examples, we looked at the early 1995 period, which was bullish for early-cycle leaders. We found that such groups as multi-line insurers, brokers, and so on, looked quite interesting. Now it is time to focus on the sell signal for insurance and buy signal for aluminums that took place in late 1993 at point

Chart 10-1　Property/casualty aluminum ratio and a long-term KST, 1985–2000. (*Source: pring.com*)

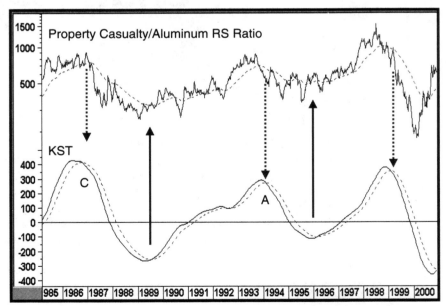

A. Since the aluminum group is our proxy for earnings-driven late-cycle leaders, the first step is to take a closer look at some of these groups.

Analysis of the Lagging Groups

Chart 10-2 shows that the RS line for the Aluminum Index broke above a downtrend line and that the RS KST gave a buy signal at the end of 1993. This was also confirmed by the absolute KST and the index itself violating a downtrend line. The breakout was soon followed by a retest of the trendline. It is important to remember that 1994 was a pretty difficult year for the market because there were two major declines at the beginning and end of the year. However, the RS line continued to zigzag up until late spring 1995.

Chart 10-3 shows that the Miscellaneous Metals Index experienced a trendline break in the RS line and an RS KST buy signal at the end of 1993. The index itself also broke above a downtrend line. This was a longer one than the violation that developed for the aluminums, so it was not surprising that the RS and absolute prices experienced a far stronger rally into

Chart 10-2   S&P Aluminum and three indicators, 1990–1996. (*Source: pring.com*)

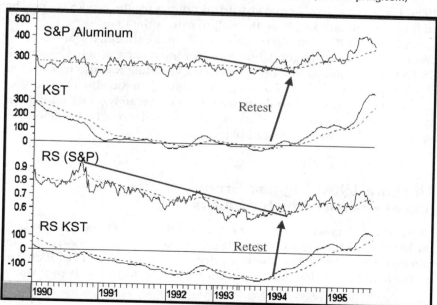

Chart 10-3   Miscellaneous Metals and three indicators, 1990–1996. (*Source: pring.com*)

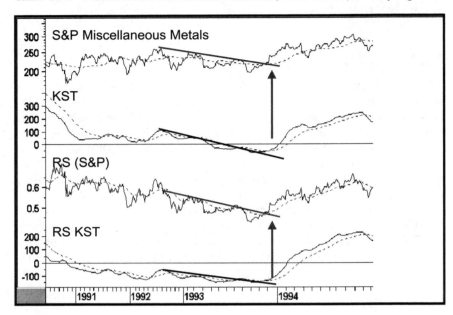

1994. It was even possible to construct trendlines for the two KSTs, thereby adding even greater weight to the bullish case at the time.

Finally, Chart 10-4 features the diversified chemicals. Once again, a trend-break in the RS line triggers a buy signal for the relative action, though the RS KST goes bullish with a delay this time. The same was also true for the absolute price and KST. The absolute KST buy signal was also a little unfortunate, in that it came when the indicator was moderately overbought. Even so, the relative and absolute price trends both performed admirably over the course of the next couple of years.

The Late 1986 Lagging Group
Signal—Semiconductor Stocks

Chart 10-1 also shows that another late cycle relative signal was given in 1986 (at point C). One group that looked attractive at the time was the aluminums (Chart 10-5). The absolute price broke out at the end of 1986, but it was not until early 1987 that the relative line and the two KSTs confirmed.

Chart 10-4 S&P Diversified Chemicals and three indicators, 1991–1997. (*Source: pring.com*)

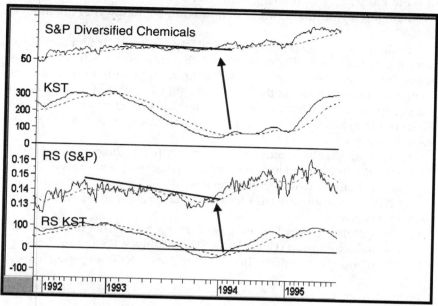

Chart 10-5 S&P Aluminum and three indicators, 1985–1988. (*Source: pring.com*)

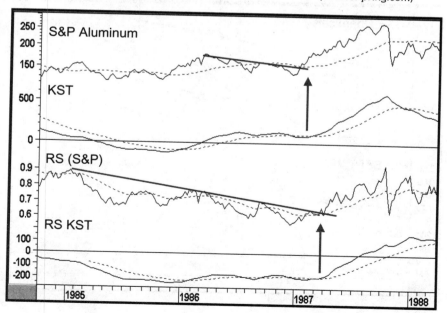

Note how the absolute and relative lines were both violated simultaneously with the EMAs, thereby offering a stronger signal. The ensuing price move was definitely worthwhile as the aluminums rallied sharply into the summer of 1987.

The chemicals group (Chart 10-6) is another late-cycle leader, but in this case, the index was well overbought by the time of the late 1986 insurance/aluminum signal. The fact that the uptrends in both the absolute and relative series were intact at the time of the signal indicated that the chemical group was a hold, but the overextended KSTs suggested that new positions could be quite risky. As it turned out, the index continued to rally for about a year.

Steels are another basic industry lagging group, but Chart 10-7 shows that the KSTs were in a more favorable position from the point of view of making a new purchase. However, the trendbreaks did not develop until early spring 1987. As a result, the advance did not take very long but was certainly quite spectacular.

Finally, technology is a lagging group, and a nice signal developed for the semiconductor group (Chart 10-8). First, it and the RS line experienced a couple of upside trendline breaks. Also, both KSTs experienced two

Chart 10-6 S&P Chemicals and three indicators, 1985–1988. (*Source: pring.com*)

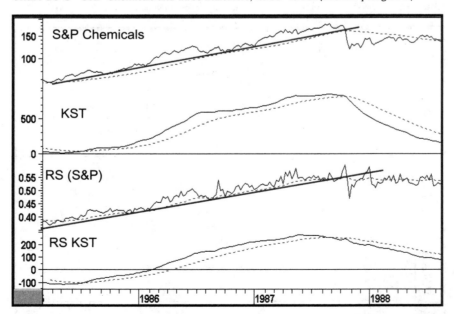

Chart 10-7 S&P Steels and three indicators, 1985–1988. (*Source: pring.com*)

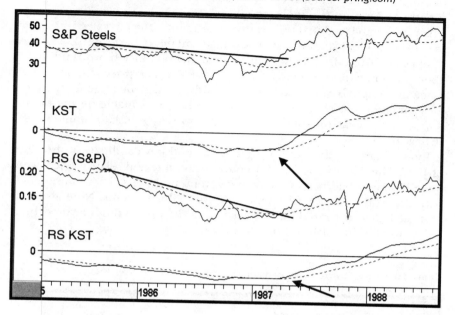

Chart 10-8 S&P Semiconductors and three indicators, 1984–1988. (*Source: pring.com*)

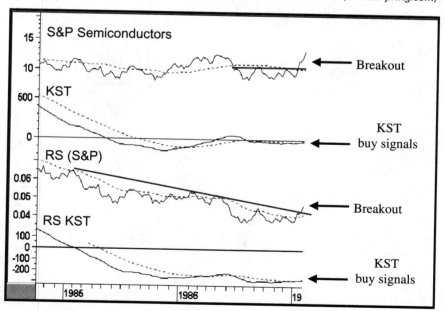

marginal KST buy signals. Chart 10-9 shows that the rally lasted about 8 months and was quite a sharp one.

Having established that the group was attractive, the next step is to examine the individual stocks; first, Texas Instruments (Chart 10-10). The best signal came from the RS line, which violated a very nice downtrend line at about the same time as it crossed above its EMA. The price also broke out. Since these signals were also associated with two KST buy signals, the technical situation was positive. This proved to be a reasonable buying opportunity, since Texas Instruments continued to rally into late summer 1987 (Chart 10-11).

Intel (Chart 10-12) also looked to be a good buy candidate at the close of 1987. The downtrend lines for both the absolute and relative prices were quite long and had been touched on several occasions. These were much better lines than those experienced by Texas Instruments. Note also that both KSTs had triggered buy signals. Thus, the probabilities favored Intel rising, which Chart 10-13 shows actually happened.

Chart 10-9   S&P Semiconductors and three indicators, 1984–1988. (*Source: pring.com*)

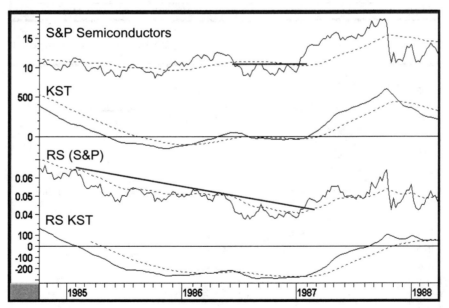

Chart 10-10   Texas Instruments and three indicators, 1983–1989. (*Source: pring.com*)

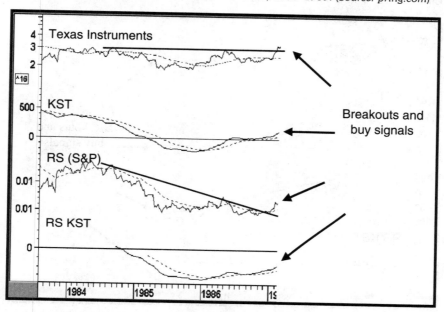

Chart 10-11   Texas Instruments and three indicators, 1983–1989. (*Source: pring.com*)

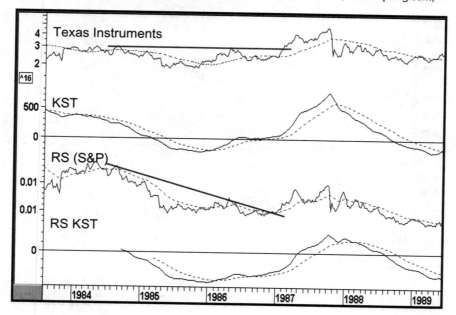

Chart 10-12   Intel and three indicators, 1983–1989. (*Source: pring.com*)

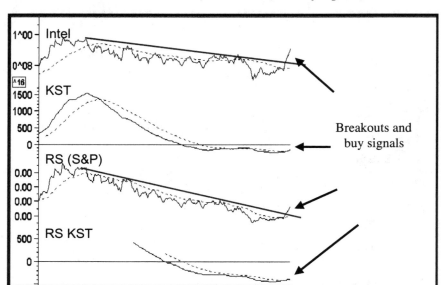

Chart 10-13   Intel and three indicators, 1983–1989. (*Source: pring.com*)

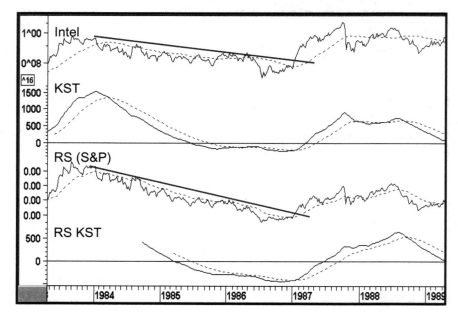

Chart 10-14   Advanced Micro and three indicators, 1984–1990. (*Source: pring.com*)

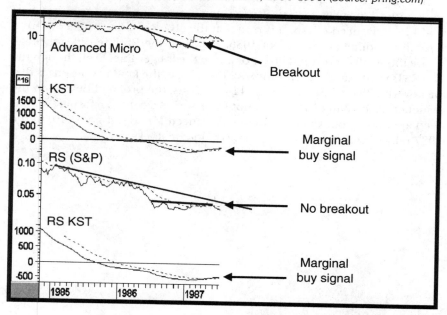

Chart 10-15   Advanced Micro and three indicators, 1984–1990. (*Source: pring.com*)

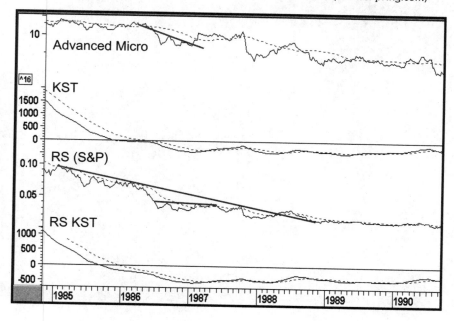

It is important to note that not all stocks benefit when a group index moves into a positive technical condition. An example is shown in Chart 10-14 for Advanced Micro. It is true that the absolute price broke out from a small trendline at the end of 1986. However, the RS line did not break above the small downtrend line, nor above the longer line. Even though the two KSTs went marginally positive, we did not get the kind of consensus that we saw with Texas Instruments and Intel. Thus, the probabilities, given the evidence at the end of 1986, did not favor such a strong performance. It is then apparent from Chart 10-15 that Advanced Micro did not share in the 1987 rally experienced by most semiconductor stocks.

11

Combining Long-Term Perspective with Short-Term Signals to Isolate Attractive Stock Candidates: I

So far, we have assumed that all industry groups fit into a nice cozy group rotation that develops around the business cycle. This is certainly true of groups that are sensitive to interest rates, such as utilities and financials, and companies that are sensitive to the tail-end of the cycle, when capacity constraints are the greatest. At this time, consumers of all types are less sensitive to price increases, meaning that earnings-driven stocks, such as basic industry, and resource sectors can quickly push those price increases to enhance the bottom line.

However, there are some groups, such as retailers, certain manufacturers, and so on, that cannot be conveniently slotted into the start or end of a business cycle. It is true, for example, that retailers do not usually emerge as leaders at the tail-end of the cycle, but sometimes they do well at the beginning and occasionally in the middle. Moreover, some groups that normally do well or badly at a particular stage in the cycle may not this time around because they are being affected by specific circumstances or factors that do not normally come into play. For example, tobaccos usually do well at the start of the cycle, but we may find that threatened changes in government policy may unduly harm the progress of these stocks. Alternatively, mining stocks generally do well at the tail-end of the cycle, but perhaps surplus capacity brought on by the excesses of previous cycles may put a lid on base metal prices, and so forth.

Whichever the case, it is important to also be able to analyze these groups on their own merit or demerit. We discussed earlier why it is of paramount importance to gain some perspective as to the direction of the main or primary trend of any security. It is fairly evident that traders or investors with a longer-term horizon need to know the direction of the primary trend, but short-term traders should, as well. A rising tide certainly lifts all boats. The same sort of principle also applies to markets, in that short-term buy signals in a primary bull market usually result in a worthwhile move. By the same token, a sell signal in a bull market is often followed by a consolidation or no decline at all. The same principle applies in bear markets, but in reverse. For example, a sell signal will usually be followed by a worthwhile shorting opportunity, whereas buy signals more often than not will result in consolidations or whipsaws rather than a good tradable opportunity. In effect—and this is extremely important to understand—*if a whipsaw is going to arise, it will invariably develop in a contratrend way*. To recap again, a primary trend is defined as lasting from as little as 9 months to 2 years, or sometimes longer.

The key, I believe, is to use guerilla warfare on the markets. By this I mean that it is not a good idea to try to identify every turn in the long-term trend of every stock or group. Rather, look for those situations where the turn is fairly obviously close to the turning point. Let me show you a couple of examples. In Chart 11-1 of First Merit Corp., there is no strong evidence of a reversal until after the price has risen about 50 percent from the low. Now it is true that we could have drawn a downtrend line for the price and observed a 65-week EMA crossover, but this is not sufficient evidence in-and-of-itself to indicate a turn of a primary trend nature. Later on, this trendbreak was confirmed by a positive signal in both the absolute and relative KSTs. This is getting closer to the kind of evidence that we need. However, it was not until the price had rallied even more that the RS line broke out from a base (Chart 11-2). The problem I have is that at no time did the price successfully test its low, thereby setting up a series of rising peaks and troughs. Conclusive evidence of a turn came only after the RS completed its base. After this point, it was safe to assume that the direction of the main trend was positive and that short-term buy signals could be used for the purpose of going long. After all, neither of the KSTs were overextended at this point. In short, the price trend reversed on a primary trend basis, but there was not sufficient evidence close to the turning point to identify an actual reversal.

Chart 11-1   First Merit Corp. and three indicators, 1987–1992. (*Source: pring.com*)

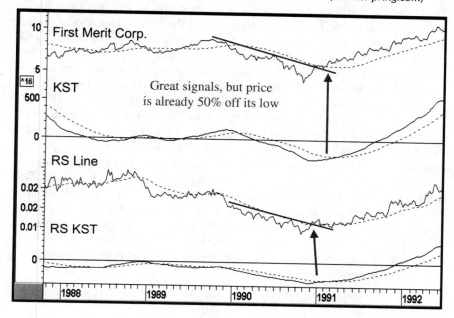

Chart 11-2   First Merit Corp. and three indicators, 1987–1992. (*Source: pring.com*)

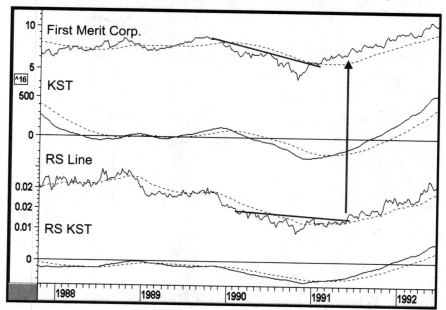

Compare that situation to the peak in General Motors featured in Chart 11-3. The first thing to notice at the upward-pointing arrow is that the RS line completes a top. There is no doubt about the fact that a series of declining peaks and troughs is now underway. The price is also well below its 65-week EMA at this point. This is closely followed by both KSTs crossing below their respective EMAs. Also, the price itself violates an uptrend line and its 65-week EMA. If any additional evidence was necessary, it soon came in the form of an upward-sloping head-and-shoulders top completion in late 1999 (Chart 11-4). Chart 11-5 focuses on the period in the rectangle in Chart 11-4 because this contains sufficient evidence to conclude that the primary trend had reversed. At this point, the KSTs had gone bearish, the RS had completed a top, and the price had violated the uptrend line. The uptrend line in Chart 11-5 represents the end of the line drawn in Chart 11-3. The solid zigzag lines represent the broad formation of rising peaks and troughs. The horizontal line indicates the point where a new trend of declining peaks and troughs was signaled. Thus, on nearly all counts, there was strong evidence that the tide had turned and that General Motors was in a bear market. From here on in, we should have been looking at opportunities from our short-term indicators to go short.

Chart 11-3   General Motors and three indicators, 1994–2001. (*Source: pring.com*)

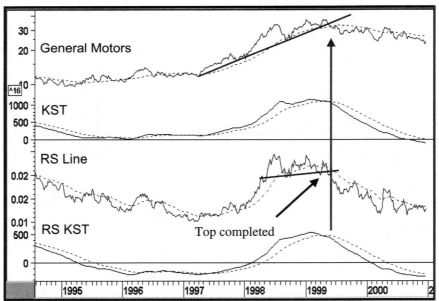

Chart 11-4 General Motors and three indicators, 1994–2001. (*Source: pring.com*)

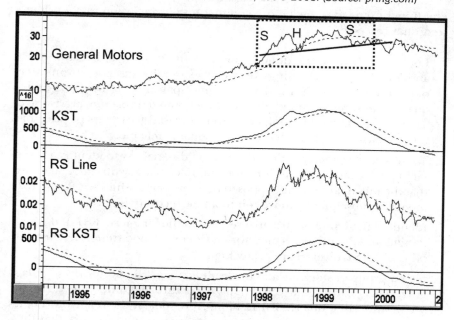

Chart 11-5 General Motors and a peak-and-trough reversal. (*Source: pring.com*)

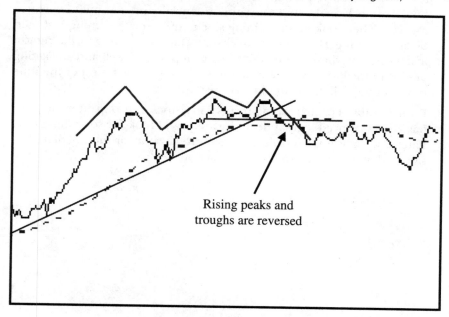

Rising peaks and
troughs are reversed

Having looked at several examples, it is now possible to summarize several things we need to see before coming to the conclusion that a primary trend has reversed.

1. Look initially for a trendline break of both absolute and relative price and/or a long-term moving-average crossover. In this case, I would recommend a 65-week EMA, that is, a time span of roughly a year-and-a-quarter. Most important of all, if you are going to use a moving average, whatever its time span, look back over at least 3 to 4 years of price history to make sure that it has been reasonably reliable.

2. To substantially increase the odds of a valid signal, try to identify a reversal in peak-trough progression. For example, in a downtrend, make sure that the initial rally off the supposed bottom is successfully tested and that the price subsequently moves on to a new recovery high.

3. Identify a flattening or an actual reversal in the long-term KST. If the KST flattens and the price it is monitoring violates a good trendline, then the odds of a KST reversal are pretty high.

4. If your group or stock fits into the leading, that is, liquidity-driven, or lagging, that is, earnings-driven groups, make sure that other indexes in the sector are acting in a similar fashion. Also, look at the relative strength and relative momentum of the opposite groups to make sure that they are acting in an opposing way. For example, if you are considering a financial stock, make sure that other financials and, say, utilities are acting well. Then look to, say, mining stocks: their relative strength should be deteriorating. Do a similar check on technology, and so forth. In most instances, you will not find all leading groups acting well and all lagging ones with weak relative strength, but you will find that most of the time most of them will be acting in a consistent way.

5. If you identify a primary trend reversal in a stock or group after the price has already moved a great deal, discard it and look for something else. Later on, when it is oversold and generates a short or intermediate buy signal, that is the time to take some action.

12

Combining Long-Term Perspective with Short-Term Signals to Isolate Attractive Stock Candidates: II

Generating Short-Term Buy Signals

There is a multitude of ways in which short-term buy signals can be generated. We cannot possibly cover them all, indeed, no one individual could possibly know all such possibilities. What I am going to do is examine several techniques that can be adapted to scan a large number of stocks. The fact that the scan turns up a particular issue is not sufficient reason to justify a purchase. *All the scan can do is let you know which stocks meet a specific technical requirement.* Let us say you are scanning for a moving-average crossover. In Chart 12-1 we see Best Buy crossing above its moving average, which is the kind of situation that a scan would have turned up. However, the crossover itself represents just one piece of evidence that the trend has

133

turned to the upside. It may be that the stock is in a bear market and is also in an overbought condition. That is exactly what happened in this situation. Chart 12-2 shows that this would have been a disastrous choice. Closer examination reveals that the price oscillator at the time was overbought, so the piece of evidence provided by the positive moving-average crossover was totally contradicted by the position of the price oscillator.

The purpose of the scan, then, is to bring likely buy candidates to your attention. It is merely a filter mechanism that should be used as a starting point for further research. My strong recommendation is that *before you do any scan using short-term criteria, do a scan for long-term criteria.* Then, when you are happy that the primary trend is up and not overextended on a long-term basis, run a short-term scan on the remaining stocks. The opposite would be true for bear trends if you are thinking of going short.

The second important point about scanning is that the scan only alerts you to a particular technical condition or set of conditions. If you like the look of the stock after further investigation, it is often then necessary to monitor it for a potential breakout or breakdown. Even those candidates that are scanned for breakout criteria need to be fully investigated to make sure they are supported by other technical criteria. For example, if the scan turns up a breakout developing from a price pattern, check to make sure that

Chart 12-1   Best Buy and a moving-average crossover, I. (*Source: pring.com*)

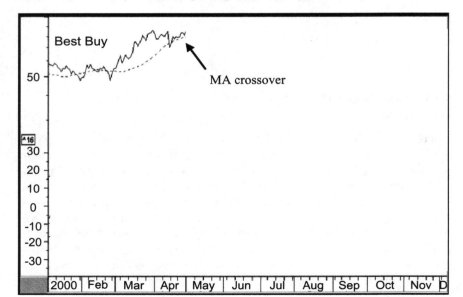

Chart 12-2 Best Buy and a moving-average crossover, II. (*Source: pring.com*)

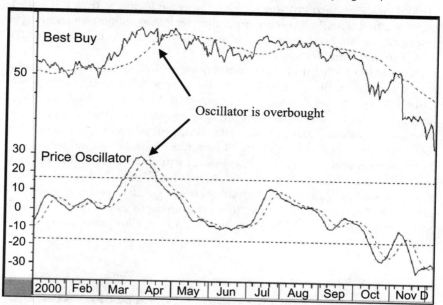

volume is expanding, and so forth. In most instances, then, the scanning process is just the starting point. The next step is to look for additional pieces of technical evidence that the stock is a good candidate, finally making decisions as to what it needs to do to qualify as an actionable situation. Only after this exercise does it make sense to pick up the phone and make that call to your friendly broker.

Short-Term Overbought/ Oversold Conditions

When establishing whether a stock is overbought or oversold, it is generally preferable to use a smoothed momentum indicator rather than a jagged one, such as a 14-day RSI. This is because the swings in the indicator, though not totally free from whipsaws, are relatively stable in their trajectory. Possibilities might include the MACD, a price oscillator (that is where an oscillator is constructed by dividing one moving average by another), my own KST, or a smoothed version of the RSI, or a rate of change.

Experience shows that none of these approaches work all the time. In fact, I would go so far as to say they are often unreliable, but at least it is a starting point. Incidentally, if you are unfamiliar with the momentum techniques described in this book, they are all explained in my double volume CD-ROM/book tutorial.[1]

The way in which I find these momentum techniques to be most useful from a buy alert point of view is to wait for the oscillator to fall below a prescribed oversold level and use the crossover of the oversold level on its way back to zero as the alert. An example is shown in Chart 12-3. This particular example uses an 8-day MA of a 9-day RSI. This smoothing approach has the advantage that it does not usually generate whipsaws. At the same time, the additional wait for an oversold crossover usually means that momentum has bottomed. After all, how else would you know that the indicator, once having moved into an oversold situation, is not going to remain there for a long time. You do not. Of course, there is nothing to stop it from whipping back below the oversold line, but the odds do not normally favor such a thing.

Chart 12-3   S&P Composite and a smoothed RSI, 1996–1997. (*Source: pring.com*)

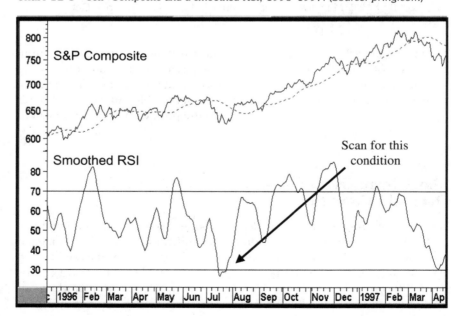

[1] *Martin Pring on Market Momentum, Volumes I and II* (pring.com).

In this exercise, the overbought zone is flagged at 70 and the oversold is at 30. Since the RSI is a momentum indicator calculated as an average to its recent past, these overbought/oversold zones can be applied to any security using this particular timeframe. RSI calculations using a longer timeframe result in a less volatile series. Consequently, had a longer time span, such as a 30-day RSI, been chosen, it would have been necessary to narrow the bands, otherwise few or no signals at all would be generated. For this example I had to pick a specific date in the past to scan for. I particularly wanted the long-term KST for the S&P to be in a bull trend to be consistent with the principles outlined earlier. This necessitated going back to summer 1996, when the RSI met our condition at the end of July. You can see from Chart 12-4 that the long-term KST was still bullish at the time, but far overextended: not an ideal situation, of course. Thus, we have our condition of a short-term buy in a long-term bull. The next series of charts will reveal some of the S&P 500 stocks that were returned from the scan.

Chart 12-4 S&P Composite and a smoothed long-term KST, 1995–2000. (*Source: pring.com*)

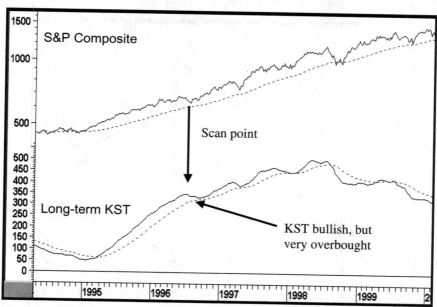

Smoothed RSI

Since the KST for the S&P was overextended, I found that almost all the stocks were in a similar position. Chart 12-5, for example, features Emerson Electric at the point where the scan was run. You can see that the KSTs were both bullish and that the price itself had fallen back to the 65-week EMA, a good support point. Chart 12-6 shows the daily action where the smoothed RSI was just coming off its oversold condition. In this case, it was possible to construct a trendline at the top of the small base at point A. This may appear to be too small a pattern on which to justify a purchase. However, one of the things that I noticed with the results of this scan was that there were not that many stocks in this position, probably because oversold conditions in bull markets are the exception rather than the rule. Normally, a price will quickly bounce off an oversold condition in a bull market, almost as if the oversold condition is too hot to touch. Consequently, a base like this is not really too small to ignore. In any event, another opportunity came along in September, as the price rallied above a more significant trendline.

Chart 12-5　Emerson Electric and three indicators, 1995–1997. (*Source: pring.com*)

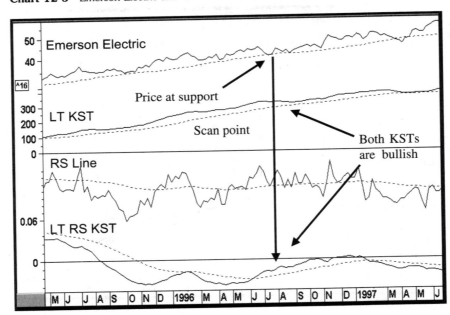

Chart 12-6 Emerson Electric and a smoothed RSI, 1996–1997. (*Source: pring.com*)

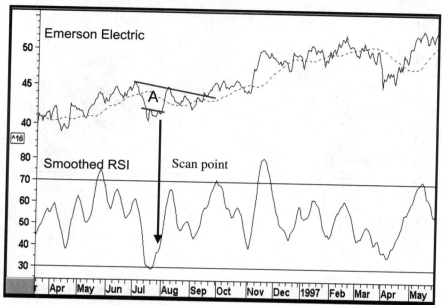

Chart 12-7 features another stock returned by the scan: Thermo Electron. As you can see, it would have been possible to buy once it crossed above the solid downtrend line. However, the stock traded sideways for a while and then dropped to a new low. It would have been liquidated as the price broke below the trendline. This was not a very successful trade, but it could have been avoided. Chart 12-8 shows why. The vertical down-pointing arrow indicates the approximate date when the scan was run. It is fairly evident that this was more of a short candidate on the next short-term rally than a buying opportunity. This is because both the absolute and relative prices had been violated by important uptrend lines and the two KSTs were rolling over.

Scanning for Favorable Long-Term Trends

Since the previous scan did not return many good long-term situations from which to launch a short-term trade, it would appear that there ought to be a better way. Why not, then, scan for a favorable long-term condition at this same period (at the end of July 1996) and filter down from there?

Chart 12-7   Thermo Electron and a smoothed RSI, 1995–1996. (*Source: pring.com*)

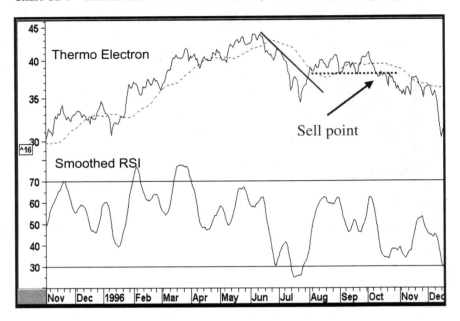

Chart 12-8   Thermo Electron and three indicators, 1995–1998. (*Source: pring.com*)

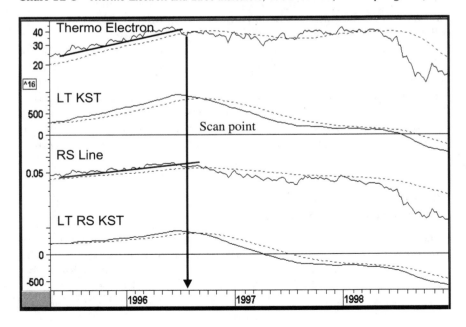

The method I chose was to scan for securities where the long-term KST was below 200 but above its 26-week EMA. If your software does not support the KST, do not worry; you could do the same exercise with a smoothed rate of change, MACD, and so forth. The main thing is to make sure that the indicator you choose reflects the long-term trend in a relatively timely manner and does not experience too many whipsaws. The scan returned a substantial number of candidates, just over 100 of the 500 stocks included in the S&P Composite.

Even so, it is still necessary to do some extensive homework with those stocks qualifying for the first round. Chart 12-9, for example, shows Central and South West. It meets our requirement where the KST is above its EMA but below the 200 level. However, both KSTs are rolling over and a sell signal is almost guaranteed, because the price and the RS line have violated important trendlines.

At the scan point for Briggs and Stratton in Chart 12-10, it is apparent that the KST is above its EMA and below 200, once again. This time, though, the RS line is below its 65-week EMA and is therefore bearish. The KST for RS is also below its EMA. It is true that the stock did rally from here, but the persistent decline in the RS line indicated that it greatly underperformed the market.

Chart 12-9 Central and South West and three indicators, 1994–2000. (*Source: pring.com*)

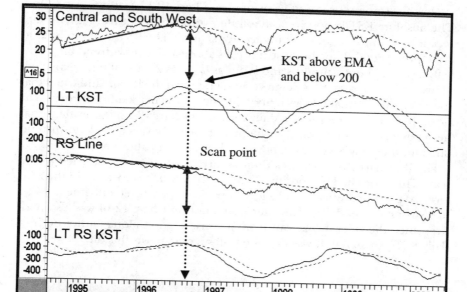

Chart 12-10   Briggs and Stratton and three indicators, 1993–2000. (*Source: pring.com*)

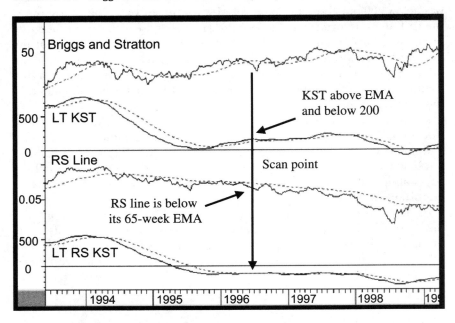

Now for some more positive examples. Chart 12-11 features Bank One. The absolute KST is positive and a little overbought, but its relative counterpart is below zero and starting to rally sharply. The RS line itself looks to be in pretty good shape because it breaks above a nice downtrend line. This rally lasts for about 6 months and is not as large as we might have expected. However, the subsequent sideways trading range in the RS line indicated that the stock's performance was in line with that of the market for the next year or so. Now, if you refer to the daily format in Chart 12-12, it is evident that here was a good entry point, as the price rallied above a 6-week downtrend line and the daily KST gave a buy signal by crossing above its MA.

Finally, Chart 12-13 features Compuware, another stock returned by the scan. This series had two positive KSTs, both of which were around the zero level, so they theoretically had a lot of upside potential. The RS line was also in a strong uptrend. The short-term situation in Chart 12-14 was also positive, since the stock broke out from a consolidation along with a positive daily KST buy signal. It was definitely all-systems-go on this one.

Chart 12-11 Bank One and three indicators, 1995–1999. (*Source: pring.com*)

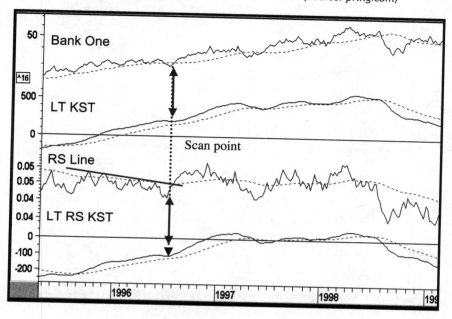

Chart 12-12 Bank One and two indicators, 1996–1997. (*Source: pring.com*)

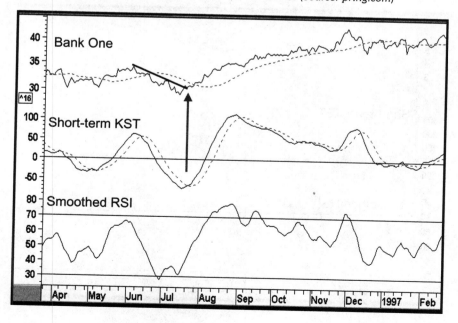

Chart 12-13 Compuware and three indicators, 1995–1998. (*Source: pring.com*)

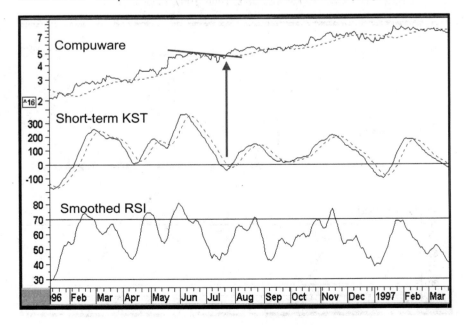

Chart 12-14 Compuware and two indicators, 1996–1997. (*Source: pring.com*)

Scanning for 52-Week New-High Breakouts

Trading market leaders as the averages are coming off a major low often provides good opportunities. Chart 12-15 shows the NASDAQ Composite around the time of the October 1998 low, just prior to one of its greatest rallies on record. Let us say we were lucky enough to identify the low. Some pointers may have included the wide media attention being given to the so-called *Asian meltdown,* far more attention, I believe, than the 1987 crash. Looking at some technical points, there was record volume a little bit after the low. Record volume is very rare, and when you see it coming off a major low, it is almost followed by a major rally. March 1979, August 1982, and the summer of 1984 attest to that. To keep the record straight, the same condition in January 2001 was not followed by a bull market. There was also a positive KST divergence, and it looked at the time of the record volume that the NASDAQ was going to rally above the downtrend line.

   With that in mind, I did a scan for technology stocks reaching a new 52-week high on October 16, just before the NASDAQ breakout. My reasoning was that a stock that could make a 52-week high so close to a major bottom ought to be in good technical shape. Having said that, there is one

Chart 12-15   NASDAQ Composite and two indicators, 1998–1999. (*Source: pring.com*)

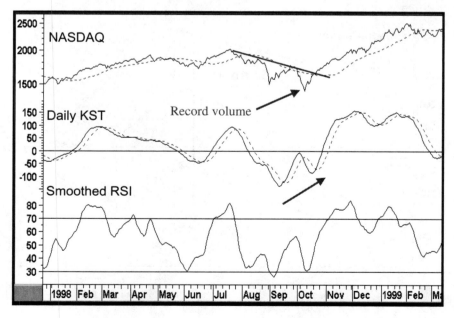
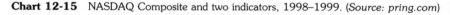

caveat: major bottoms are often associated with a *change* in leadership. We obviously need to identify the new leaders, not the old ones.

Watson Pharmaceutical (Chart 12-16) had been a stellar performer during the mini–bear market. However, at the time of the scan, the long-term KST was extremely overbought. There was no reason why the price could not extend its advance, but the probabilities favor the new leadership rather than the old. As you can see, the price did rally, but not for long, as it and its RS line both violated trendlines and the two KSTs gave sell signals. In a situation such as this, it is usually better to select a stock that has been in a trading range during the preceding decline and then starts to break on the upside. An example developed with Solectron at the time of the October scan. Chart 12-17 shows that it was possible to construct two trendlines, both of which experienced breakouts. The two KSTs were also marginally above their EMAs at the time of the scan. This was not a perfect situation because the KST at the time of the scan was moderately overbought. I would prefer to see a longer trading range and a lower KST level, but we do not always get everything we are looking for. Chart 12-18 also indicates a breakout above a resistance trendline that is accompanied by a short-term KST buy signal. Consequently, both the long- and short-term situations are in a positive mode.

Chart 12-16   Watson Pharmaceutical and three indicators, 1996–2001. (*Source: pring.com*)

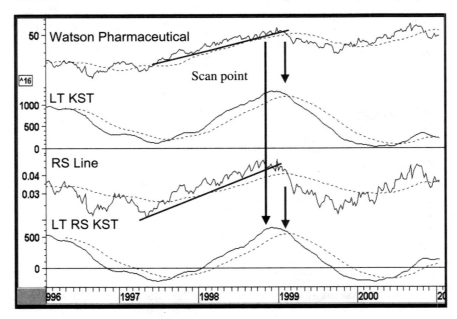

Chart 12-17 Solectron and three indicators, 1996–2001. (*Source: pring.com*)

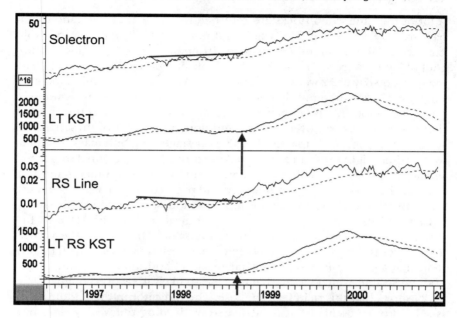

Chart 12-18 Solectron and two indicators, 1998–1999. (*Source: pring.com*)

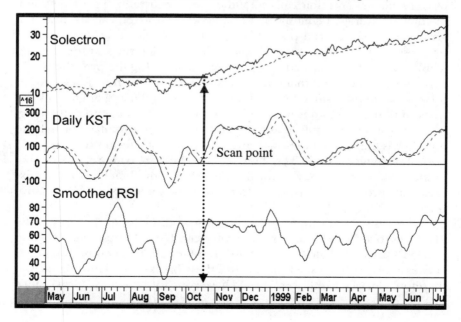

Waiting for Pull-Backs

A lot of the time when stocks are returned from a scan, a substantial rally has already taken place. This would not normally be true of a scan involving a reversal of a smoothed oscillator from an oversold condition, but it could be if we were scanning for a breakout situation, such as a stock reading a new 30-day or 52-week high, and so on. Alternatively, we might be scanning for weekly or monthly data using a moving-average crossover of a long-term smoothed momentum indicator: this, too, could return a stock that is in a short-term overbought condition. Since a lot of these types of scans will return stocks that are in the early stages of a bull market, should we buy them right there and then, looking through any potential short-term setbacks, or should we wait for the correction? My feeling is that in most situations, the stock should be monitored and purchased later, when the short-term situation is closer to equilibrium or a modest oversold condition.

Chart 12-19 features the long-term technical position of ADC. In this instance, the buy-point returned from the scan is flagged by the vertical arrow, that is, where the two KSTs have just turned positive. It is fairly evident that a good rally has already taken place, both for the absolute price and the RS line, which means that the stock is likely to be overbought. Chart 12-20 shows that this is, in fact, the case. The indicator in the middle panel is a 1/13 price oscillator. It is calculated by dividing the weekly close by a 13-week moving average. The lower panel features another intermediate price oscillator. This time, it is smoother because it reflects a 10-week simple moving average being divided by a 26-week MA. You can see from the arrow denoting the scan point at the end of February that the smoother price oscillator was overbought. Thus, while the long-term picture suggested a bull market, the intermediate situation was signaling the probability of a correction. It is evident that one did take place over the next few weeks. In this case, as in most situations of this nature, it would have paid to stalk the stock until the conditions were right for a purchase. Remember, the long-term situation is still bullish at this point. The other advantage of stalking the stock is that during the corrective phase, the long-term situation could possibly turn bearish. The key, then, is to use the scan to identify good long-term, low-risk situations, wait for the correction, and then buy on the next breakout, provided the primary trend of both the absolute and relative prices are still bullish.

In this case, the buying opportunity comes a bit later in the year, as the price falls to its EMA following a brief whipsaw. Then the absolute price and the 1/13 price oscillator break above trendlines. The smoother oscillator crosses above its MA just a little bit after these breaks. This latter signal was, therefore, delayed a little, but I would have gone with the trendbreaks, since

Chart 12-19 ADC and three indicators, 1995–2001. (*Source: pring.com*)

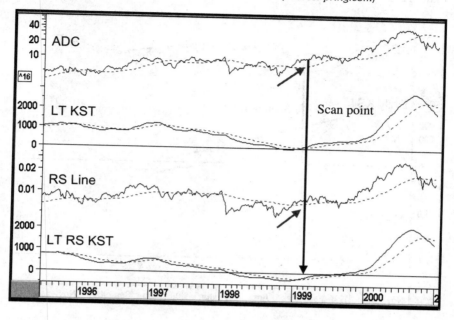

Chart 12-20 ADC and two indicators, 1997–2001. (*Source: pring.com*)

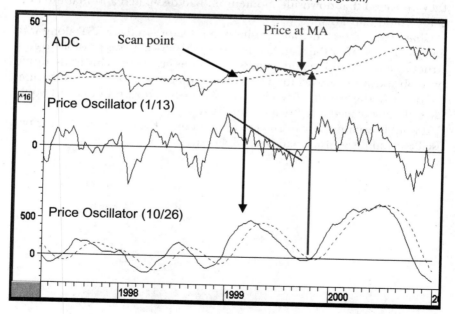

Chart 12-21   ADC and two indicators, 1998–2000. (*Source: pring.com*)

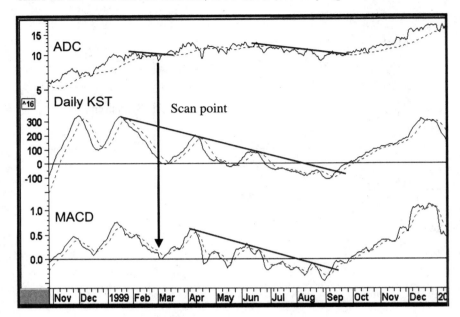

they indicated that downside momentum had dissipated and that the indicator would rally anyway.

Chart 12-21 shows the daily position and features a daily KST along with an MACD. Just after the scan had returned this stock, it was possible to construct a small trendline and witness an upside breakout. This trade would have obviously been okay for a short-term swing trade, but the overbought condition in the two 10/26-week price oscillators in the previous chart would have already placed a red flag on the field.

It would certainly have been better to wait until the trendlines for the two oscillators and the price had been violated.

Appendix
Stock Selection from a Secular Point of View

General

It makes sense to start off from a very long term, or secular, point of view, gradually working down to the short-term aspects. Ideally, the selection process should begin by determining whether the stock in question is in a secular advance or decline to gain some idea of where the stock might be in its ownership cycle. Chart A-1 shows Cominco, a Canadian mining company, which went through many cycles between the 1970s and the turn of the century. Stocks in resource and basic industries, such as Cominco, are called *cyclical* stocks, since they offer great profit opportunities over one or two business cycles but are rarely profitable using the buy-hold approach.

Because of the long-term growth characteristics of the global economy, most stocks exhibit characteristics of a long-term secular advance interrupted by mild cyclical corrections or multi-year trading ranges.

An example is shown in Chart A-2, featuring Alberto Culver. Several secular trends are evident. The termination of the first is signaled by a joint trendline break in the price and the RS line in 1991. You may notice that the trendline for the RS is penetrated very briefly in 1985. Some might regard this as sacrilege, but I prefer to construct trendlines that best reflect the trend in a commonsense way, rather than one that joins the low with the initial corrective bottom. If it is possible to do that and the line can also

Chart A-1   Cominco, 1970–2001 *Telescan*. (*Source: pring.com*)

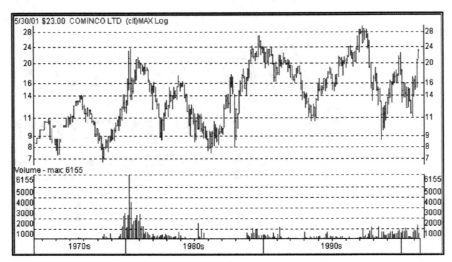

Chart A-2   Alberto Culver, 1982–2001. (*Source: pring.com*)

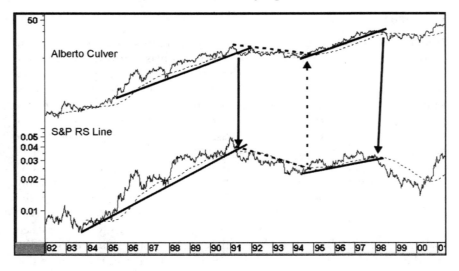

be touched on more occasions, that is fine. However, if it is not, as would have been the result in this case, then it makes more sense to make an exception and construct the line through one of the bottoms, instead of just touching it. Later on, we see a couple of 4-year downtrend lines violated and in 1998 the penetration of two uptrend lines. Both moving averages have a 104-week (24-month) time span and are penetrated at around the same time as the trendlines.

I have incorporated the RS line into most of the charts in this Appendix for two reasons. First, RS trends and divergences can be very helpful in understanding the strength or weakness in the underlying technical structure. Second, when a stock is purchased, it is far better for it to be in a trend that is outperforming, rather than underperforming, the market. Chart A-3 offers a classic example of this. During the 20-year period covered by the chart, Reliant Energy was in a secular uptrend. This looked good on the surface, but a quick glance at the RS line indicates that it was in a secular downtrend in terms of relative performance. Note that it was possible to construct two trendlines for the price. The dashed one is an extremely good example of why it is a good idea to extend a trendline, once it has been violated. Note how the extended line became formidably resistant several times in the mid-to-late 1990s. Even when the price broke above the line at the turn of the century, the retracement move found support there.

Finally, ADM experiences a secular break to the downside in 1998 (Chart A-4). Its RS line also completed a downward head-and-shoulders top. Note that in ADM's case, advance warning of potential weakness was given first by the failure of the RS line to confirm the new high in the price in 1995 (at the tip of the horizontal arrow) and then to diverge negatively with the late 1997 high.

Chart A-3 Reliant Energy, 1980–2001. (*Source: pring.com*)

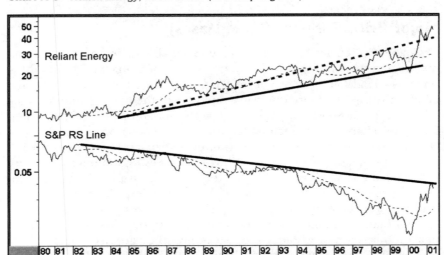

Chart A-4   ADM, 1980–2001. (*Source: pring.com*)

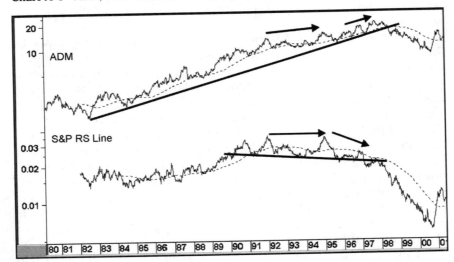

These examples point out the differing life cycles and characteristics of individual stocks. Investors who are able to identify secular trend reversals in price and relative action are in a position to profit from extremes in the ownership cycle. Consequently, a very long term chart can provide a useful starting point for stock selection.

Major Price Patterns (Long Bases)

In Chapter 5 on price patterns, the relationship between the size of the formation and the ensuing price move in terms of both magnitude and duration was established. The bigger the base, the further they can race! Or, the greater the top, the more they will drop! One of the best methods of stock selection for those with a patient long-term horizon is to search through long-term chart books (such as the SRC Green Book, www.babson.com/charts/longterm.html) or your own downloaded database for issues that are emerging from, or pulling back to, long-term bases. By definition there are few points in a stock's lifetime when this condition is prevalent, but when it can be spotted, it is well worthwhile. At any one time, there are usually at least a few of these situations developing. When it is possible to spot a lot of candidates simultaneously forming large bases, this usually means that the market as a whole, or the stock group or groups in question, is on the verge of a secular advance. In the late 1940s and the late 1970s, for

Chart A-5   Andrew Corporation, 1980–2001. (*Source: pring.com*)

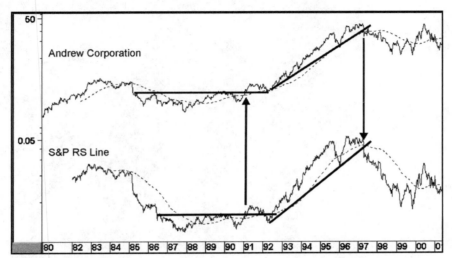

example, there were numerous stocks breaking out from multi-year bases. Not surprisingly, the market itself experienced a strong secular advance in both instances.

Chart A-5 shows an example for Andrew Corporation breaking out from a 6-year base in 1991. A good rally, more than meeting the objective of the pattern, followed. Later on, the joint penetration of a 6-year uptrend line indicated that the strong uptrend was unlikely to continue. In the case of the price, this was followed by a consolidation, and for the RS line, an actual trend reversal. Applied Materials experienced a breakout from a 10-year base in late 1992. The uptrend in the price continued until at least spring 2001, but the RS uptrend line was temporarily violated in 1998 and 2000.

Index

About the Author

Martin J. Pring is the highly respected president of Pring Research (**www.pring.com**), editor of the newsletter *The Intermarket Review,* and one of today's most influential thought leaders in the world of technical analysis. Pring has written more than a dozen trading books and has contributed to *Barron's* and other national publications. He was awarded the Jack Frost Memorial Award from the Canadian Technical Analysts Society.

Introduction to the Critically Acclaimed *Technical Analysis Explained*, 4/e by Martin J. Pring

To investors willing to buy and hold common stocks for the long term, the stock market has offered excellent rewards over the years in terms of both dividend growth and capital appreciation. The market is even more challenging, fulfilling, and rewarding to resourceful investors willing to learn the art of market timing through a study of technical analysis.

The advantages of this approach over the buy-and-hold approach were particularly marked between 1966 and 1982. The market made no headway at all, as measured by the Dow Jones Industrial Average (DJIA), in the 16 years between 1966 and 1982. Yet there were some substantial price fluctuations. Although the DJIA failed to record a net advance between 1966 and 1982, the period included five major advances totaling over 1500 Dow points. The potential rewards of market timing were therefore significant.

A long-term investor fortunate enough to sell at the five tops in 1966, 1968, 1973, 1979, and 1981 and to reinvest the money at the troughs of 1966, 1970, 1974, 1980, and 1982 would have seen the total investment (excluding transactions costs and capital gains tax) grow from a theoretical $1000 (that is, $1 for every Dow point) in 1966 to over $10,000 by October 1983. In contrast, an investor following a buy-and-hold approach would have realized a mere $250 gain over the same period. Even during the spectacular rise that began in August 1982, technical analysis would have proved useful, since that period witnessed a considerable variation in performance between different industry groups.

A bull market, such as the one that occurred in the 1980s and 1990s, is a once-in-a-generation affair. In fact, it was a record in 200 years of recorded U.S. stock market history. This implies that the opening decade of the twenty-first century will be a more difficult and challenging period, and that market timing will prove to be of crucial importance.

In practice, of course, it is impossible to buy and sell consistently at exact turning points, but the enormous potential of this approach still leaves plenty of room for error, even when commission costs and taxes are included in the calculation. The rewards for identifying major market junctures and taking the appropriate action can be substantial.

Originally, technical analysis was applied principally in the equity market, but its popularity has gradually expanded to embrace commodities, debt instruments, currencies, and other international markets. In the days of the old market, participants had a fairly long time horizon, stretching over months or years. There have always been short-term traders and scalpers, but the technological revolution in communications has shortened the time horizon of just about everyone involved in markets. When holding periods are lengthy, it is possible to indulge in the luxury of fundamental analysis, but when time is short, timing is everything. In such an environment, technical analysis really comes into its own.

To be successful, the technical approach involves taking a position contrary to the expectations of the crowd. This requires the patience, objectivity, and discipline to acquire a financial asset at a time of depression and gloom, and liquidate it in an environment of euphoria and excessive optimism. The level of pessimism or optimism will depend on the turning point. Short-term peaks and troughs are associated with more moderate extremes in sentiment than longer-term ones. The aim of this book is to explain the technical characteristics to be expected at all of these market turning points, particularly major ones, and to help to assess them objectively.

Technical Analysis Defined

During the course of the book when it is time to emphasize a specific but important point, it will be highlighted in the following way:

> **Major Technical Principle** Technical analysis deals in probabilities, never certainties.

The technical approach to investment is essentially a reflection of the idea that prices move in trends that are determined by the changing attitudes of investors toward a variety of economic, monetary, political, and psychological forces. The art of technical analysis, for it is an art, is to *identify a trend reversal at a relatively early stage and ride on that trend until the weight of the evidence shows or proves that the trend has reversed.* The evidence in this case is represented by the numerous *scientifically* derived indicators described in this book.

Human nature remains more or less constant and tends to react to similar situations in consistent ways. By studying the nature of previous market turning points, it is possible to develop some characteristics that can help to identify market tops and bottoms. Therefore, *technical analysis is based on the assumption that people will continue to make the same mistakes they have made in the past.* Human relationships are extremely complex and never repeat in identical combinations. The markets, which are a reflection of people in action, never duplicate their performance exactly, but the recurrence of similar characteristics is sufficient to enable technicians to identify juncture points. Since no single indicator has signaled, or indeed could signal, every top or bottom, technical analysts have developed an arsenal of tools to help isolate these points.

Three Branches of Technical Analysis

Technical analysis can be broken down into three essential areas: sentiment, flow-of-funds, and market structure indicators. Data and indicators for all three areas are available for the U.S. stock market. For other financial markets, the statistics are more or less confined to the market structure indicators. The major exceptions are futures markets based in the United States, for which short-term sentiment data are available. The following comments on sentiment and flow-of-funds indicators relate to the U.S. stock market.

Sentiment Indicators

Sentiment or expectational indicators monitor the actions of different market participants, such as insiders, mutual funds managers and investors, and floor specialists. Just as the pendulum of a clock continually moves from one extreme to another, so the sentiment indexes (which monitor the emotions of investors) move from one extreme at a bear market bottom to another at a bull market top. The assumption on which these indicators are based is that different groups of investors are consistent in their actions at major market turning points. For example, insiders (that is, key employees or major stockholders of a company) and New York Stock Exchange (NYSE) members as a group have a tendency to be correct at market turning points; in aggregate, their transactions are on the buy side toward market bottoms and on the sell side toward tops.

Conversely, advisory services as a group are often wrong at market turning points, since they consistently become bullish at market tops and bearish at market troughs. Indexes derived from such data show that certain readings have historically corresponded to market tops, while others have been associated with market bottoms. Since the consensus or majority opinion is normally wrong at market turning points, these indicators of market psychology are a useful basis from which to form a contrary opinion.

Flow-of-Funds Indicators

The area of technical analysis that involves what are loosely termed flow-of-funds indicators analyzes the financial position of various investor groups in an attempt to measure their potential capacity for buying or selling stocks. Since there has to be a purchase for each sale, the *ex post*, or actual dollar balance between supply and demand for stock, must always be equal. The price at which a stock transaction takes place has to be the same for the buyer and the seller, so naturally the amount of money flowing out of the market must equal that put in. The flow-of-funds approach is therefore concerned with the before-the-fact balance between supply and demand, known as the *ex ante relationship*. If at a given price there is a preponderance of buyers over sellers on an ex ante basis, it follows that the actual (ex post) price will have to rise to bring buyers and sellers into balance.

Flow-of-funds analysis is concerned, for example, with trends in mutual fund cash positions and those of other major institutions, such as pension funds, insurance companies, foreign investors, bank trust accounts, and customers' free balances, which are normally a source of cash on the buy side. On the supply side, flow-of-funds analysis is concerned with new equity offerings, secondary offerings, and margin debt.

This money flow analysis also suffers from disadvantages. Although the data measure the availability of money for the stock market (for example, mutual fund cash position or pension fund cash flow), they give no indication of the inclination of market participants to use this money for the purchase of stocks, or of their elasticity or willingness to sell at a given price on the sell side. The data for the major institutions and foreign investors are not sufficiently detailed to be of much use, and in addition they are reported well after the fact. In spite of these drawbacks, flow-of-funds statistics may be used as background material.

A superior approach to flow-of-funds analysis is derived from an examination of liquidity trends in the banking system, which measures financial pressure not only on the stock market, but on the economy as well.

Market Structure Indicators

This area of technical analysis is the main concern of this book, embracing *market structure* or the *character of the market indicators*. These indicators monitor the trend of various price indexes, market breadth, cycles, volume, and so on in order to evaluate the health of the prevailing trend.

Indicators that monitor the trend of a price include moving averages, peak-and-trough analysis, price patterns, and trendlines. Such techniques can also be applied to the sentiment and flow-of-funds indicators discussed previously. This is because these indicators also move in trends. When the trend of psychology, as reflected in these series, reverses, prices are also likely to change direction.

Most of the time, price and internal measures, such as market breadth, momentum, and volume, rise and fall together, but toward the end of market movements, the paths of many of these indicators diverge from the price. Such divergences offer signs of technical deterioration during advances, and technical strength following declines. Through judicious observation of these signs of latent strength and weakness, technically oriented investors are alerted to the possibility of a reversal in the trend of the market itself.

Since the technical approach is based on the theory that the price is a reflection of mass psychology, or the crowd in action, it attempts to forecast future price movements on the assumption that crowd psychology moves between panic, fear, and pessimism on one hand and confidence, excessive optimism, and greed on the other. As discussed here, the art of technical analysis is concerned with identifying these changes at an early phase, since these swings in emotion take time to accomplish. Studying these market trends enables technically oriented investors and traders to buy or sell with a degree of confidence in the principle that once a trend is set in motion, it will perpetuate itself.

Classification of Price Movements

Price movements may be classed as primary, intermediate, and short term. *Major movements*, sometimes called *primary* or *cyclical*, typically work themselves out in a period of 1 to 3 years and are a reflection of investors' attitudes toward the business cycle. *Intermediate movements* usually develop over a period of 6 weeks to as many months, sometimes longer. Although not of prime importance, they are nevertheless useful to identify. It is clearly important to distinguish between an intermediate reaction in a bull market and the first downleg of a bear market, for example. *Short-term movements,* which last less than 3 or 4 weeks, tend to be random in nature. Secular or very long term trends embracing several primary trend movements and intraday trends lasting a few minutes to a few hours round out the possibilities for price movements.

Discounting Mechanism of the Market

All price movements have one thing in common: *They are a reflection of the trend in the hopes, fears, knowledge, optimism, and greed of market participants.* The sum total of these emotions is expressed in the price level, which is, as Garfield Drew noted, "never what they [stocks] are worth, but what people think they are worth."[1]

This process of market evaluation was well expressed by an editorial in *The Wall Street Journal*:[2]

> The stock market consists of everyone who is "in the market" buying or selling shares at a given moment, plus everyone who is not "in the market," but might be if conditions were right. In this sense, the stock market is potentially everyone with any personal savings.
>
> It is this broad base of participation and potential participation that gives the market its strength as an economic indicator and as an allocator of scarce capital. Movements in and out of a stock, or in and out of the market, are made on the margin as each investor digests new information. This allows the market to incorporate all available information in a way that no one person could hope to.

[1]Garfield Drew, *New Methods for Profit in the Stock Market*, Metcalfe Press, Boston 1968, p. 18.
[2]The *Wall Street Journal*, Oct. 20, 1977. Reprinted by permission of the *Wall Street Journal*. Copyright Dow Jones & Co., Inc. 1977. All rights reserved.

> **Major Technical Principle**   The market never discounts the same thing twice.

Since its judgments are the consensus of nearly everyone, it tends to outperform any single person or group. . . . [The market] measures the after-tax profits of all the companies whose shares are listed in the market, and it measures these cumulative profits so far into the future one might as well say the horizon is infinite. This cumulative mass of after-tax profits is then, as the economists will say, "discounted back to present value" by the market. A man does the same thing when he pays more for one razor blade than another, figuring he'll get more or easier shaves in the future with the higher-priced one, and figuring its present value on that basis.

This future flow of earnings will ultimately be affected by business conditions everywhere on earth. Little bits of information are constantly flowing into the market from around the world as well as throughout the United States, and the market is much more efficient in reflecting these bits of news than are government statisticians. The market relates this information to how much American business can earn in the future. Roughly speaking, the general level of the market is the present value of the capital stock of the U.S.

This implies that investors and traders are looking ahead and taking action so that they can liquidate at a higher price when the anticipated news or development actually takes place. If expectations concerning the development are better or worse than originally thought, then investors sell either sooner or later through the market mechanism, depending on the particular circumstances. Thus, the familiar maxim *sell on good news* applies on when the *good* news is right on or below the market's (that is, the investors') expectations. If the news is good, but not as favorable as expected, a quick reassessment will take place, and the market (other things being equal) will fall. If the news is better than anticipated, the possibilities are obviously more favorable. The reverse will, of course, be true in a declining market. This process explains the paradox of equity markets peaking when economic conditions are strong, and forming a bottom when the outlook is most gloomy. The principle of discounting is not confined to equities alone, but can be applied to *any* freely traded entity.

The reaction of any market to news events can be most instructive because if the market, as reflected by price, ignores supposedly bullish news and sells off, it is certain that the event was well discounted, that is, already built into the price mechanism, and the reaction should therefore be viewed bearishly. If a market reacts more favorably to bad news than might be expected, this in turn should be interpreted as a positive sign. There is a good deal of wisdom in the saying, "A bear argument known is a bear argument understood."

The Financial Markets and the Business Cycle

The major movements in bond, stock, and commodity prices are caused by long-term trends in the emotions of the investing public. These emotions reflect the anticipated level and growth rate of future economic activity, and the attitude of investors toward that activity.

For example, there is a definite link between primary movements in the stock market and cyclical movements in the economy because trends in corporate profitability are an integral part of the business cycle. If basic economic forces alone influence the stock market, the task of determining the changes in primary movements would be relatively simple. In practice, it is not, and this is due to several factors.

First, changes in the direction of the economy can take some time to materialize. As the cycle unfolds, other psychological considerations, such as political developments or purely internal factors like a speculative buying wave or selling pressure from margin calls, can affect the equity market and result in misleading rallies and reactions of 5 to 10 percent or more.

Second, changes in the market usually precede changes in the economy by 6 to 9 months, but the lead time can sometimes be far shorter or longer. In 1921 and 1929, the economy turned before the market did.

Third, even when an economic recovery is in the middle of its cycle, doubts about its durability often arise. When these doubts coincide with political or other adverse developments, sharp and confusing countercyclical price movements usually develop.

Fourth, profits may increase, but investors' attitudes toward those profits may change. For example, in the spring of 1946 the DJIA stood at 22 times the price/earnings ratio. By 1948, the comparable ratio was 9.5 when measured against 1947 earnings. In this period, profits had almost doubled and price/earnings ratios had fallen, but stock prices were lower.

Changes in bond and commodity prices are linked much more directly to economic activity than are stock market prices, but even here, psycho-

> **Major Technical Principle** These basic principles of technical analysis apply to all securities and time frames from 20-minute to 20-year trends.

logical influences on price are very important. Currencies do not fit well into business cycle analysis. Although data reported several months after the fact are very good at explaining currency movements, technical analysis has been most useful for timely forecasts and the identification of emerging trends.

Technical Analysis and Trend Determination

Since technical analysis involves a study of the action of markets, it is not concerned with the difficult and subjective tasks of forecasting trends in the economy, or assessing the attitudes of investors toward those changes. Technical analysis tries to identify turning points in the *market's* assessment of these factors.

Since technical analysis can be applied successfully to any freely traded entity such as stocks, market averages, commodities, bonds, currencies, and so on, I will frequently use the term *security* as a generic one embracing all of these entities, thereby avoiding unnecessary repetition.

The approach taken here differs from that found in standard presentations of technical analysis. The various techniques used to determine trends and identify their reversals will be examined in Part I, "Trend-Determining Techniques," which deals with price patterns, trendlines, moving averages (MAs), momentum, and so on.

Part II, "Market Structure," is principally concerned with analysis of the U.S. equity market, although examples using other securities are included to demonstrate that the principles are universally applicable. All that is required are the appropriate data. This section offers a more detailed explanation of the various indicators and indexes. It also shows how they can be combined to build a framework for determining the quality of the internal structure of the market. A study of market character is a cornerstone of technical analysis, since reversals of price trends in the major averages are almost always preceded by latent strength or weakness in the market structure. Just as a careful driver does not judge the performance of a car from the speedometer alone, so technical analysis looks further than the price trends of the popular averages. Trends of investor confidence are responsible for price movements, and this emotional aspect is examined from four viewpoints or dimensions, namely, price, time, volume, and breadth.

Changes in prices reflect changes in investor attitude, and *price*, the first dimension, indicates the level of that change.

Time, the second dimension, measures the recurrence and length of cycles in investor psychology. Changes in confidence go through distinct cycles, some long and some short, as investors swing from excesses of optimism toward deep pessimism. The degree of price movement in the market is usually a function of the time element. The longer it takes for investors to move from a bullish to a bearish extreme, the greater the ensuing price change is likely to be. The examples in the two chapters on time relate mainly to the U.S. stock market, but much of this material is equally valid for commodities, bonds, or currencies.

Volume, the third dimension, reflects the intensity of changes in investor attitudes. For example, the level of enthusiasm implied by a price rise on low volume is not nearly as strong as that implied by a similar price advance accompanied by very high volume.

The fourth dimension, *breadth*, measures the extent of the emotion. This is important because as long as stocks are advancing on a broad front, the trend in favorable emotion is dispersed among most stocks and industries, indicating a healthy and broad economic recovery and a widely favorable attitude toward stocks in particular. On the other hand, when interest has narrowed to a few blue-chip stocks, the quality of the trend has deteriorated, and a continuation of the bull market is highly suspect.

Technical analysis measures these psychological dimensions in a number of ways. Most indicators monitor two or more aspects simultaneously; for instance, a simple price chart measures both price (on the vertical axis) and time (on the horizontal axis). Similarly, an advance/decline line measures breadth and time.

Part III, "Other Aspects of Market Behavior," deals with more specialized aspects. These include interest rates and the stock market, sentiment, automated trading systems, individual stock selection, and technical analysis as applied to global markets.

Conclusion

Financial markets move in trends caused by the changing attitudes and expectations of investors with regard to the business cycle. Since investors continue to repeat the same type of behavior from cycle to cycle, an understanding of the historical relationships between certain price averages and market indicators can be used to identify turning points. No single indicator can ever be expected to signal all trend reversals, so it is essential to use a number of them together to build up a consensus.

This approach is by no means infallible, but a careful, patient, and objective use of the principles of technical analysis can put the odds of success very much in favor of the investor or trader who incorporates these principles into an overall strategy.

THE INTERMARKET REVIEW

is a 34+ page monthly publication which will keep you current on the U.S. Bond, stock, and precious metal markets. Each issue also contains up-to-date information on currencies, international debt, equity markets and commodity indices.

This is the only source that uses Martin's 6-Stage Business Cycle approach. The business cycle has seasons just like a calendar year. Each of the six distinct stages, or seasons, can be used to create new investment opportunities and reap their profits. The InterMarket Review identifies these stages and explains how they will affect your portfolio. Martin provides specific asset allocation recommendations, along with market developments you need to be aware of.

EVERY MONTH YOU WILL RECEIVE IN-DEPTH COVERAGE OF:

- Martin's personal Barometers for the Bond, Stock and Commodity markets. These unique indicators have identified all major turning points in the postwar period, usually on a very timely basis and have outperformed the buy/hold approach by a wide margin.

S&P Composite and the Stock Barometer

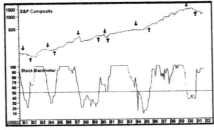

Barometers help organize the economic data that recognize

- Chart Watch - features the market Martin feels is poised for a major move.

- Pring Turner Stock Report - insights from Joe Turner of Pring Turner Capital Group, on a stock they are monitoring for their portfolio considerations.

- Martin's Personal Portfolio Recommendations - Every issue has at least 6 stocks Martin feels are a potential purchase. Long- and short-term charts are here, along with buy recommendations!

Backed by over 30 years of Martin's personal technical experience providing analysis for key brokerage firms, developing indicators, investing in markets and learning from the past, you're sure to find the InterMarket Review educational and informative.

*Please visit **www.pring.com** to sign up for a 3-month trial and view an issue!*

Name
_____

Address
_____

_____

_____

City
_____

State and Zip/Postal
_____

Country
_____

Telephone
_____

E-mail

Pring Research, Inc.
1539 S. Orange Avenue
Sarasota, FL 34239
800-221-7514   941-364-5850

Installation Instructions

This CD has an Autorun feature. Insert the CD into the CD-ROM drive and it will start automatically. Please allow sufficient time for loading.

If the Autorun feature does not work, insert the CD, open your CD-ROM drive and double-click on the Setup.exe icon. Then, access the program by clicking on Start, Programs, Pring and locate the icon for the tutorial title you are playing in the flyout.

1. We recommend not changing the default installation settings.
2. This program is best veiwed using small fonts.
3. This CD is best viewed in 800 × 600 pixels and 256 colors.
4. For additional support, please go to Support at **www.pring.com**.

Advanced Technical Analysis CD Tutorials:
Learning the KST
Intro to Candlestick Charting
Tech's Guide to Day Trading
Breaking the Black Box
How to Select Stocks

MetaStock CD Tutorials:
Exploring MS Basic
Exploring MS Advanced
Super CD Companion
Indicator Companion
Market Analysis Companion
Selecting Stocks Using MetaStock

*Visit **http://www.pring.com** for info on these and other products.*

Pring Research, Inc.
1539 S. Orange Avenue, Sarasota, FL 34239
800-221-7514 • 941-364-5850
Internet: www.pring.com • E-mail: info@pring.com